"Whether you're angry or sad about the breakup, *Befriending Your Ex after Divorce* shows you how to manage your feelings and find healthy new ways to relate to your ex. A valuable guidebook that should be read by everyone who has an ex!"

—Constance R. Ahrons, PhD, author of *The Good Divorce* and *We're Still Family*

"*Befriending Your Ex after Divorce* is a wise, practical, and compassionate guide that will help make your transition easier, happier, and ultimately a pathway to renewal. It is a gateway into forgiveness—which is the key to all lasting change. This is a must-read for anyone going through a divorce with children."

—Barbara Biziou, author of *The Joy of Ritual* and *The Joy of Family Rituals*

"This is an inspiring book that every divorced parent should have on their night table, and every therapist who works with divorcing families should have it in their office. Judith Ruskay Rabinor offers both a professional and personal model of co-parenting that nurtures emotional connection with oneself, as well as emotional communication with one's ex. Her work is based on a deep understanding of the importance of maintaining healthy attachment bonds, for the sake of both children and parents, alike.

—Diana Fosha, PhD, founder and director of the AEDP Institute

"I highly recommend this book to anyone who truly wants to get along with their ex—as well as to those who have no interest in being friends. Every page is full of well-researched information that can help even the most jilted of spouses relate to their ex in a way that holds the best interest of the children as a top priority and promotes healing for everyone involved. It should be mandatory reading for anyone whose marriage is ending."

—Susan Pease Gadoua, LCSW, author of *Contemplating Divorce* and *Stronger Da*

"One of the hardest things we are called upon to do in life is to open our hearts to someone who hurt or betrayed us. Yet therapists deal every day with the tragic consequences to divorced families when the exes keep feuding and stewing. *Befriending Your Ex after Divorce* helps former partners access the love and compassion they have for each other that is buried beneath the pain. The post-divorce life of families doesn't have to be barren and bitter. This book can help make it a period of learning and beauty."

—Richard Schwartz, PhD, founder and director of Internal
Family Systems and author of *Introduction to Internal Family
Systems Therapy* and *You Are the One You've Been Waiting For*

"Judith Ruskay Rabinor is a clinical psychologist who has felt the pain of divorce herself and helped hundreds of clients through those trials. If you are facing a painful break-up or have experienced one, or if you simply want to help someone who has, this book is for you. Abraham Lincoln said, 'Am I not destroying my enemies when I make friends of them?' Now, here is Rabinor's accumulated wisdom on this topic. She aims at not just helping you minimize pain, but enlisting an ally. You can draw on her wisdom in this book if you want to help make life more peaceful and productive for your children, yourself, and your ex."

—Everett L. Worthington, Jr., author of
Forgiving and Reconciling (InterVarsity Press)

"In my over 35 years as a practicing divorce attorney at Jenner & Block, I have seen too many divorcing couples act out grudges with their exes in destructive post-divorce conflicts. Much has already been written to minimize these outcomes by explaining the importance of having a good divorce for the sake of the children, and proposing strategies for co-parenting after divorce. Rabinor's book, however, goes deeper and offers a fresh perspective by focusing on the couple's personal relationship after divorce…. A groundbreaking perspective, certain to reframe our thinking on post-divorce life."

—James. H. Feldman, Esq, family law partner and board chair
of The Family Institute at Northwestern University

"Divorce ends a marriage; it doesn't end a family…. This book teaches separated spouses how to let go of the anger, grief, and resentment that prevents them from getting on with their lives."

—Melinda Blau, author of fourteen books, including
Families Apart: Ten Keys to Successful Co-Parenting and
award-winning journalist

"This book is an invaluable resource for divorcing parents who want their children to grow up healthy and emotionally secure in a dual-household family. Rabinor's insight, experience, humor, and spunk make her one of my favorite experts to interview for my films."

—Leta Lenik, documentary film producer whose films
include *Hungry to be Heard* and *Women Unchained*

"Rabinor's book compels us to remember what we all know deep down inside: being good parents and role models to our children is the most important life purpose. While it may be human to carry the hurt and disappointment of a failed marriage, it is our job to protect our children from our experiences. Letting go will not only be good for our children, but for us and our exes as well. Read this book and spare yourself unnecessary time, grief, and legal fees. Take her advice and you will learn to manage your relationship with your former spouse in a healthy, productive manner."

—Wendy Hoey Scheinberg, Esq

"Judith Ruskay Rabinor has written a guide to divorce that is sensitive while offering tough advice; seemingly overly optimistic yet realistic for those able to take the long view of divorce. I recommend this book especially to divorcing parents and the professionals who work with them."

—Robert E. Emery, PhD, director of the Center for Children,
Families, and the Law, University of Virginia

"Before you hire an aggressive attorney, read this book. Save not only for your child's college education fund but for the emotional strength and sanity of your entire family!"

—Judge Irene Sullivan, ret., author of *Raised by the Courts: One Judge's Insight into Juvenile Justice*

"'Ex' and 'friend' usually equate with 'impossible' in the minds of most divorcing or divorced couples. Yet, after reading Rabinor's book, the impossible not only seems quite possible, but inevitable. Using compassionate, yet compelling tone, Rabinor provides a much-needed bridge for couples to get even the angriest of exes to understand the importance of an amicable co-parenting relationship and how to actually put the understanding into constructive action. Truly a must-read for anyone facing a separation/divorce or who has already gone through one. Rabinor shows us that it's never too late to heal from divorce!"

—Debra Mandel, PhD, author of *Dump That Chump: From Doormat to Diva in Only Nine Steps*

befriending your ex after divorce

making life better
for you, your kids,
and, yes, your ex

JUDITH RUSKAY RABINOR, PhD

NEW HARBINGER PUBLICATIONS, INC.

Publisher's Note

Distributed in Canada by Raincoast Books

Copyright © 2012 by Judith Ruskay Rabinor
New Harbinger Publications, Inc.
5674 Shattuck Avenue
Oakland, CA 94609
www.newharbinger.com

Acquired by Melissa Kirk; Cover design by Amy Shoup;
Edited by Nelda Street; Text design by Tracy Marie Carlson

Library of Congress Cataloging-in-Publication Data

Rabinor, Judith Ruskay, 1942-
  Befriending your ex after divorce : making life better for you, your kids, and, yes, your ex / Judith Ruskay Rabinor.
     p. cm.
  Includes bibliographical references.
  ISBN 978-1-60882-277-5 (pbk. : alk. paper) -- ISBN 978-1-60882-278-2 (pdf e-book) -- ISBN 978-1-60882-279-9 (epub) 1. Divorced people. 2. Divorce. 3. Divorced parents. I. Title.
  HQ814.R25 2013
  306.89--dc23

                          2012033500

Printed in the United States of America

14 13 12   10 9 8 7 6 5 4 3 2 1   First printing

Dedicated to
Arnold J. Rabinor
(1944–2012)

My ex-husband, Arnold J. Rabinor, passed away as this book was going to press. Until his untimely death, I counted our relationship as one of the most significant, long-term relationships in my life. We divorced in 1983, when our children were eight and twelve, and created a family based in two homes. As co-parents, we shared the minutiae of everyday life, as well as the important milestones: we cheered at gymnastics and swim meets, celebrated birthdays and graduations, and, later on, weddings and the birth of grandchildren. Although it wasn't seamless and there were bumps in the road, we remained committed to co-parenting. This commitment shaped my life. May his memory be a blessing and remind you that even if your marriage fails, it's possible to keep your family together.

Contents

foreword

Although a great many books have been written to help soothe a divorcing couple's wounds and spare their children, the ex-spousal relationship has been sadly neglected. The surprising discovery that ex-spouses can have positive, meaningful, and supportive relationships with one another is sorely missing from popular and professional literature. *Befriending Your Ex after Divorce* helps to fill that gap. Judy Rabinor's ability to write as both a divorced person and a psychologist makes her uniquely positioned to integrate research, clinical practice, and the everyday reality faced by a divorced parent. Story after story—including Judy's own story—reminds the reader that once the tsunami of divorce quiets down, exes can be friends who share a major joy: loving and raising their children and grandchildren.

Befriending Your Ex after Divorce is a brave and beautiful book that challenges destructive myths about divorce and creates a plan for a new divorce consciousness. It's a forward-looking book, one that helps recontextualize divorce in a new climate, one that acknowledges grief, loss, and trauma because doing so helps divorced parents to separate while allowing them to remain connected to the family they have created and the children they love.

Professionals should read this book too. It should be in the library of psychotherapists, educators, clergy, lawyers, and family-court judges: all of the people who help families through the difficult process of divorce. The excellent suggestions and superb practical exercises in this book will foster new attitudes and behaviors, both for divorcing couples and for the professionals who can be of so much help. Professionals have a powerful role to play in educating the public about the need for a new divorce mind-set. Because too many divorce lawyers still promote a down-and-dirty approach to their practices and too many mental health professionals hide behind a screen of anonymity rather than remind parents that child rearing is a mutual responsibility, hearing this message is urgent. For professionals who read it, this book is sure to spark ideas about how to work in the light and with integrity.

Divorce is always difficult and often traumatic. In my forty years as a practicing clinical psychologist working with families and couples, and especially as an expert on infidelity, I have learned the power and importance of letting go, one of Judy's most important themes.

There's a distinction between letting go and forgiving. Letting go is a private matter that's at the heart of healing. When we harbor angry and bitter feelings, those feelings eat away at our well-being and have a profound effect on us and those closest to us: our children, family, and friends, as well as on the next relationship. Even without a partner's genuine remorse, letting go is possible. But without profound remorse, forgiveness is not really achievable, and in the wake of divorce, many people are not necessarily genuinely remorseful. It's not necessary to forgive someone who is not genuinely remorseful, but it's important to let go of the toxic feelings. What's important is that we let go of the past, forgive when appropriate, and stay focused on the present befriended relationship: on current actions, deeds, and intentions that can strengthen befriending and benefit all who are involved.

Letting go is not about pretending things are other than they are. It's about facing the ghastliness of what happened, and giving you and your ex an opportunity to share your mutual sadness. Most people who marry (or become a monogamous couple) accept the implicit promise of "Till death do us part." Sharing this sadness may help the divorcing couple accept that each partner was part of the problem and can be part of the solution, charting a successful future as co-parents who share responsibilities as well as the happy and sad occasions in the life of the family that they created. From this point, new doors can then open that allow for fresh beginnings. Judy's exercises on letting go, showing compassion, and forgiving can help people get beyond their anger. I am happy to see that she is not afraid to integrate spirituality into psychotherapy.

While a marriage may be brief, divorce lasts a lifetime. Fortunately for us all, Judy has provided a compassionate, insightful, and comprehensive guide to light the way toward forgiveness and friendship. In examining befriending and its ramifications for your life, I hope you will one day participate in one of the befriending celebrations that Judy has created in this book.

—Don-David Lusterman, PhD
author, *Infidelity: A Survival Guide*

acknowledgments

This book would never have been written without the support of many relationships. First and foremost, I want to extend a special thank-you to my patients, as well as innumerable friends and strangers who have generously shared their lives with me.

I'd especially like to thank Karen Propp, PhD, who began as a consulting editor and has become my collaborator and friend: thank you for helping me shape this project from the beginning of my journey, for helping me create and sustain a vision, and for supporting me at every stage.

I'd also like to thank my agent, Claire Gerus, for her ongoing support, positive energy, determination, and devotion.

I am fortunate to have had the support of several people at New Harbinger Publications. In particular, Melissa Kirk has been involved in the development of this book from the beginning through the final word: thank you for your encouragement, enthusiasm, patience, and consistent availability. Additional thanks go to Jess Beebe and Nelda Street, who helped smooth out the rough edges in a magical way.

My thanks to many friends and colleagues: Marion Bilich and Didi Goldenhar, my first writing group; Judith Brisman and Natasha Prenn, who listened while I dreamed and who read many early drafts of chapters. Thanks to Richard Zuckerberg and Esther Altmann, who encouraged me to follow my dream, and to April Lane Benson, who helped me find just the right title.

This book would never have come to be without my befriended ex, Arnie Rabinor, with whom I cocreated and lived a "befriended relationship" even before that term existed in my imagination. Thanks also to our children, Zachary Rabinor and Rachel Rabinor.

Finally, I'd like to thank my husband, Larry Wetzler, for the ongoing love, support, inspiration, and music he has brought into my life during this long and arduous writing process.

introduction

Marriages end when the pain of staying together seems worse than the pain of divorce—at least that's how my marriage ended. After fifteen years of marriage and two children, neither my ex-husband nor I wanted to break up our family, and yet our marriage was unraveling. Staying together became impossible. We tried everything: we went to individual and couples therapy, and took weekend retreats; we took romantic vacations and spent time apart. We talked to friends, family, and one another. Nothing helped, and eventually we divorced.

As a clinical psychologist, I have worked with hundreds of families struggling with the aftermath of divorce. So I bring to this book my professional and personal experience. Divorce does not have to destroy your children, batter your soul, or rob you of years of quality living. While many divorced couples are resigned to being bitter enemies with little that's positive to say to or about one another, I believe that these couples and their children are losing out. While divorce is often a trauma, it does not have to be a lifelong sentence to misery. Befriending your ex is about living with what lingers and learning to make peace with your life as it is now.

Anyone touched by divorce can gain help and understanding from this book, but it's primarily aimed at parents—biological and adoptive—who are separated, divorcing, or divorced. If you and your ex-partner were never legally married but are committed to co-parenting, you will benefit as well. The term "divorced" includes all separated, committed parents, whether heterosexual or same-sex.

Divorce ends a marriage but not the parenting relationship between a pair of biological or adoptive parents, or stepparents. The divorce literature consistently stresses that co-parenting is a profound responsibility; what's new about this book is the idea that divorce is also an opportunity to develop a new, healthy, and healing relationship with your ex. While it may seem counterintuitive to do so, you may find that once your divorce is finalized, you can build a new, meaningful parenting relationship with the person you once married and divorced. Your co-parenting relationship may be a springboard to a deeper connection. Over and over, I have witnessed exes becoming allies once the initial pain and anguish of divorce have ebbed. In fact, once the legalities are finalized, the ex-spousal relationship can intensify in positive ways. One reason I'm writing this book is to offer a guide to this process.

Pioneering the Good Divorce

I divorced in 1983, when I was forty, after being married for fifteen years. My daughter was eight, and my son twelve. When I was growing up in the fifties and sixties, I hardly knew anyone whose parents were divorced, but I did know that children of divorce—from "broken homes," the pejorative term applied to divorced families—usually lived with their mothers. So imagine my surprise when my soon-to-be ex-husband calmly said to me, "Why should the kids live with you and I get them only on weekends? Maybe they should live with me during the week and you on the weekends."

The children live with him? I was stunned. He argued that as a real-estate developer with his own business who worked at home on a flexible schedule, he was the more available parent than I was, as a psychologist who worked at an office during fixed hours. As he rattled on, I began hyperventilating: my heart was pounding, my hands sweating. Now I understand that these are normal physiological reactions to feeling overwhelmed, panicky, and terrified. Divorce brings with it a series of losses, and I was absorbing and experiencing this reality in my body.

Once I got over my initial panic, I realized that my soon-to-be ex was serious about wanting to parent our children after the divorce. He truly wanted to co-parent. Hesitantly, I began to consider his proposal. After a great deal of negotiation, my ex and I arrived at a compromise: our children would live half the time with him and half the time with me in what is now known as a *binuclear family*: a family that resides in two separate homes (Ahrons 1994). We were pioneering what is now a more conventional arrangement for divorcing parents: *joint physical custody*.

At the time of our divorce, I could never have imagined that I would develop a relationship with my ex that would become supportive and comforting, even friendly. But over time, that's exactly what happened. When we first separated and were newly divorced, it wasn't that way. We were distant, sometimes aloof, and often wary of one another. Yet for the most part, we were able to use "in the best interest of the children" as our guiding "North Star."

We quickly learned to collaborate around the myriad issues involved in our children's daily routines. Together, we attended school conferences and sat in the bleachers, cheering at children's swim meets and gymnastic competitions. We collaborated to help the children resolve problems large and small concerning school, homework, friends, and our family life. We celebrated their birthdays together and slowly began to establish new ways of celebrating other holidays. As time went on, we became more trusting and comfortable with each other, including new partners and eventually new spouses in family events. More recently, we danced at our children's weddings, cried at the funerals of each other's parents, and welcomed grandchildren. All this occurred over many years and not without many painful moments.

What I have learned, from my own experience and from counseling others, is that although befriending your ex is a complex process filled with potholes, pitfalls, and glitches, it's more satisfying and attainable than you may realize. While I'm not grateful I divorced, I am grateful to be connected to the man who fathered my children, shared in raising them, and remains as committed to them as I am. For this reason, too, I wrote this book to offer guidance and hope to the next generation of divorcing families.

My Professional Training

I became a psychologist over thirty-five years ago. Seeking to understand how people can live richer lives has been a lifelong passion of mine. In the past decades, after studying many schools of thought, I developed an eclectic approach, integrating ideas from psychoanalytic theory, family systems, feminist thinking, neurobiology, and diverse experiential and spiritual traditions. At the core, I am grounded in the pioneering work of Jean Baker Miller (1976) and Carol Gilligan (1982), and the philosophy of the Stone Center at Wellesley College, which proposes a view of psychological development known as *relational-cultural theory* (Miller 1976). This theory posits the healing power of being in relationship and the damaging impact of isolation. My work and my life are grounded in the belief that growth-fostering relationships are a central human necessity. Helping people develop deeper connections to themselves (to their deepest thoughts, feelings, and desires), to other people (family and friends), and to every resource the universe offers (spirituality, nature, creativity, and so on) is my mission.

Recent developments in brain research have validated this basic premise: human beings are hardwired to connect (Goleman 2006). Just as we need air, food, and water to live, we thrive when we are in relationship—with ourselves and others. This concept is particularly relevant to anyone who is divorced or considering divorcing. Although divorce ends a legal relationship, it need not sever emotional attachments that may continue to be a lifelong source of sustenance. Just because two people can't sustain the rigors and demands of marriage doesn't mean they can't befriend one another.

The love that you and your ex share for your children is a unique bond and connection, one that can be fostered for the betterment of all involved. My goal is to help divorcing parents access—in the midst of the pain of divorce—their love, to create new family units that can facilitate the personal growth of all family members. A family unit may be located in two separate homes and may not meet the criteria of the traditional family, yet, nonetheless, can be a family that offers nourishment, nurturance, support, and connection.

The Interviews

When I started this book, little had been written about exes who befriend one another, so I reached out to my network of personal and professional friends, and websites. A series of interviews provided me with an incredible amount of data. (See the appendix for the interview questions.)

While writing the book, I had the privilege of speaking to dozens of people who define themselves as "befriended" exes. I conducted traditional face-to-face interviews and gathered material by e-mail and telephone.

What took me by surprise as I interviewed these strangers was my own personal journey. Listening to stories of heartbreak and resilience evoked my own feelings about my divorce story. My own emotional reaction often reminded me of the old saying: "No tears for the writer, no tears for the reader" (Frost 1972, 440). The sheer volume of people with a burning desire to talk about their divorces with me, a complete stranger, amazed me. During the interview process, participants were often choked with emotion, in awe at how moved and tearful they were while looking back at their journeys. Common responses included "I didn't realize how much baggage I still carry from my divorce" and "Thank you for helping me look at this dark period in my life once again."

I learned several lessons from these interviews. First, even a good divorce contains an incredible amount of pain, sadness, and even trauma. Divorce is always a serious rupture in one of the most important of all human connections: marriage. A profound attachment disruption, divorce brings with it multiple and ongoing wounds and losses. Issues of rejection, betrayal, humiliation, and a sense of failure are the norm. Second, the human spirit is amazingly resilient. People do get over the pain of divorce. Third, getting over the pain of divorce is not the same thing as forgetting. Most people never totally heal their most painful wounds, and divorce, more likely than not, falls into the category of a profoundly painful wound. And fourth, my interviews confirmed one of my deepest beliefs: long-term attachments have incredible value. Many people I interviewed expressed not only concern for their former spouses, but also relief that they had managed to foster a new connection, no matter how tenuous, with their exes. This, in itself, was one of the outstanding findings of my research: the hunger for connection is lifelong, and anger, animosity, and resentment can be overcome.

All spiritual traditions confirm the psychological principle that human connectedness built on compassion, forgiveness, collaboration, and mutual support gives us a sense of well-being. Recent MRI findings (Goleman 2006) corroborate this as well; for example, small acts of altruism—something as simple as helping an elderly person cross a street—are found to activate hormones, such as endorphins and oxytocin, that release warmth, energy, and a sense of well-being. This phenomenon, known as the "helper's high," confirms what helpers and healers have always known: helping others helps the helper as well as the sufferer. Befriending your ex has the possibility of helping and healing *you*, your children, and, yes, your ex!

How to Use This Book

Each chapter in this book offers stories, information, and strategies to address the emotional aspects of life most affected by divorce. Take your time as you read; you may want to reread some sections several times. In addition, I strongly encourage you to keep a journal to process your emotions thoroughly. The physical act of writing can help you absorb your experience in a unique and beneficial way that differs from talking or thinking about it.

Not every exercise in this book will apply to you, but many will. Many of the exercises are meant to guide you in examining your own thoughts, feelings, and behaviors; some exercises require you to respond to questions and assess your own behavior. These self-assessments will help you identify trouble spots that you need to work on in the reparative exercises or assignments that follow the self-assessments. Track your progress by keeping a journal. Reviewing your journal as often as you wish will help you assess your strengths, liabilities, and growth.

The strategies in this book have been designed to offer you tools, coping skills, and opportunities for personal growth and healing. Healing is unique: one size does not fit all, and different strategies work for different people at different times. At times of stress, some people calm down using mindfulness meditation; others are able to use guided imagery to access safety or positive images; some call a friend; and others access a calm, peaceful state using deep breathing, journal writing, or reading. My goal is to offer you a wide variety of skills, techniques, and strategies that will help you manage the roller coaster of events, situations, and emotions that will be evoked as you negotiate your divorce and work toward befriending your ex.

As a therapist, I've learned how difficult it is to change and how much we all need to practice stretching. The exercises in this book will offer you innumerable opportunities to stretch your emotional and psychological muscles. The strategies, guidelines, and exercises that I suggest are based on a simple principle: the bedrock of emotional growth is the capacity to take risks. Befriending your ex is choosing to take a risk. Opening this book is a risk. Congratulate yourself! I am grateful to accompany you on this journey of renewal.

CHAPTER 1

what does it mean to befriend your ex?

Given that you are reading this book, chances are you are divorced or contemplating divorce. Chances are you have come across divorced people, like Helena, who have developed a collaborative relationship with their exes:

> *Thanksgiving at our house is a very special event. My husband and I love everything about the holiday rituals, from setting up to shopping for food and cooking. And I look forward to seeing everyone who comes—not just Robbie, my ex, but also Lynn, my husband's ex, and her current husband. They all contribute delicious family recipes. The children—ours, his, hers—all look forward to being together. It's such a warm and fun holiday. Of course, it wasn't always that way, but now Thanksgiving is something we all look forward to every year.*

You probably would like to have a better relationship with your ex. You might even still have some warm feelings for the person with whom you were once in love. You might know divorced couples who celebrate Thanksgiving together or sit on the bleachers cheering their children's home runs. You may be looking for support or confirmation, because you have been developing a friendship with your ex about which others have been disparaging or critical. You may be wondering how to break out of a stalemated relationship with your ex. Or, you may be feeling hostility, anger, or resentment toward your ex but realize that you will need to have a good co-parenting relationship so that your kids can enjoy a positive relationship with both of you. It might just be that you are curious about the whole concept of befriending your ex.

In writing this book, I have been amazed at how many people are delighted that I am validating the concept that becoming friends with your ex makes life better: for you, your kids, and, yes, your ex. It's common knowledge that when divorced parents get along, children benefit. The converse is a given too: parental conflict damages children. But few books talk about the benefits of befriending your ex, for not only the children, but also you and, yes, your ex.

Befriending Your Ex expands and extends the concept of co-parenting after divorce that so many contemporary books endorse. I believe that the relationship that divorced parents develop with one another is important in its own right. Yet this relationship, which can be lifelong, nourishing, and even affectionate, is not talked or written about much.

What Befriending Is

Stereotypical tales of bitter divorces and their ensuing endless warfare have affected most of us. We have taken our cues about how ex-spouses behave and feel toward their exes from popular movies and stories, such as *The Second Wives Club* (Moore 2006), in which a group of divorced female friends feel empowered and find pleasure in seeking revenge on their exes. Yet what I've experienced in my personal life and learned in my office is that many divorced people can and do form a friendly, supportive, and communicative relationship with their exes.

Befriending takes time and effort. It may involve going through unique periods of darkness and pain, but you can accomplish it if you are truly committed to doing so. Helena, whose story began this chapter, had been divorced nearly a decade before the joyous, commingled Thanksgiving celebrations came about.

The circumstances under which your marriage ended are very relevant to your relationship going forward and to the steps you will need to take to develop a befriended relationship. It's clearly more difficult to befriend your ex-husband if you divorced because he was having an affair when you were pregnant than if your children are grown and you divorced because you both realized you had simply grown apart. It's easier to befriend an ex who left when both your careers were established than to befriend an ex who was unemployed, ran up astronomical debt on the credit cards, and dragged you through an ugly legal battle.

Through the lens of statistics, divorce is a commonplace event. However, seen through the lens of emotion, divorce can be a shock, a crisis, and even a traumatic event. Keep in mind that people's responses to getting divorced range from "Ho hum, so I guess this isn't working out" to "Oh my god, this is a trauma and I can't cope!" The intensity and duration of your emotional responses to your divorce also depend on your personality, your resiliency, any history of loss and trauma, and the responses of those close to you. If you have children, the chances of divorce becoming traumatic greatly increase if you fail to collaborate in the divorce process, and decrease when you and your ex are able to communicate openly with each other and your children about the numerous situations, events, and stresses you will inevitably face in the wake of divorce.

The Binuclear Family

In her book *The Good Divorce: Keeping Your Family Together When Your Marriage Comes Apart*, Constance Ahrons (1994), noted family therapist and author, coined the term "the binuclear family." She defined this new family unit as any family spanning two or more households. Each parent has a private sphere in her home and whenever the children are with her. Parents also share a collaborative space where they intersect that consists of when they attend school events, talk about decisions that affect their children's daily life and larger issues surrounding education or health, and attend important occasions, such as birthdays, graduations, and weddings. Children are encouraged to develop full relationships with each of their parents and often, but not always, spend comparable amounts of time in Mom's house and Dad's house. Parents may remarry and introduce new partners into their private spheres, but the concept of a binuclear family remains. Befriending your ex is central to the peaceful workings of a binuclear family.

The concept of a binuclear family is different from that of a "blended family." A blended family, which has its own issues, comes about when a couple sets up a household with children from previous marriages; in this scenario, stepparents and stepsiblings must learn to form new relationships with one another. A binuclear family is a family with two "nuclei": an original family has split and continues their relationships under new understandings and circumstances, with a unique structure.

Ahrons (ibid.) found that 50 percent of the couples she interviewed had formed an amicable relationship with their exes within two to three years of the initial separation. She spelled out the necessary characteristics of a good divorce:

- Both the adults and children emerge at least as emotionally well off as they were before the divorce.

- A family remains a family. The rights of the children are respected, and both parents continue to be responsible for the emotional, economic, and physical needs of their children.

Ahrons found that many parents had developed excellent working relationships with not only their former spouses, but also their former spouses' new partners.

Befriending Is about Developing a New Relationship

Befriending your ex-spouse is about forming a new and positive relationship that is different from the one you had as a married couple (Blau 1993). It's about starting over, making a conscious, mindful, deliberate effort to let go of past hurts, wounds, and beliefs. This new relationship is likely to begin when you focus on the best interests of your children, and it will continue to include emphasizing goodwill, collaboration, and cooperation (Emery 2004) as you and your ex navigate the specific details of your life and your children's lives. You can develop a befriended relationship with your ex regardless of whether you have a joint-custody agreement or a more traditional agreement, in which one parent has sole custody and the other has visitation rights. What's important is the quality of the relationship, what I call a commitment to the *five "c's" of befriending*: communication, collaboration, compromise, compassion, and celebration. Here are some examples of how the five "c's" manifest in a befriended relationship:

- *Communication:* You call your ex to let him know you will be twenty minutes late when dropping off the kids on Friday afternoon. When you get there, you explain that your middle schooler has to finish working on a big school project due on Monday.

- *Communication, compromise, compassion:* Your ex wants you to share the cost of a new bicycle for your child that you feel is too expensive. You tell your ex the amount that you feel comfortable contributing to this purchase, and your ex agrees to make up the difference.

- *Compassion:* Your ex is recuperating from a broken leg, so you shop for groceries and drop them off at her house.

- *Collaboration, celebration:* You and your ex plan a graduation party for your child and invite both your and his new families.

- *Compassion, collaboration:* You turn to your ex, a financial wizard, for help with figuring out the economics of arranging care for your elderly mother, who suffers from dementia.

What Befriending Is Not

Befriending your ex is not about retaining the intimacy you once had as a married couple. You can no longer expect to know the details of how your ex spends her time and money, or whom she sees. You can no longer expect her to be available to you 24/7. You can no longer rely on her for emotional support for the events in your life that don't involve the children. Nor can you micromanage how she cares for the children. Although you may find that your ex can be emotionally supportive, this shouldn't be a given. Your ex is probably not your best friend. Your physical, or sexual, connection is over, even if, at times, you feel sexually attracted to one another. And—this may be the hardest one—although you may often have angry feelings toward your ex, you no longer have the right to act on them. Although we can't always control our emotions, we can control our actions, and now, it's up to you to control your behavior.

Throughout this book I will present exercises to help you develop this difficult yet crucial skill.

Why Befriend Your Ex?

Here are some common responses from people who think befriending your ex can't work:

- "Why would I want to befriend that womanizer?"

- "After what she did to me?"

- "That liar and thief? I could never trust him again!"

While your ex may have caused you grief in the past, befriending your ex is about giving both of you another chance—not for your marriage, but for a new, postdivorce relationship.

For Your Children

Because you and your ex share children, you have created a bond that is far stronger than anything that could be broken by a signature on a divorce decree. Regardless of your custody agreement, you won't be able to excise your ex from your life forever. That's because your ex is your child's parent forever. One of the most important and consistent research findings regarding the adjustment of children to divorce is that children who have two involved parents adjust to divorce far easier than those who do not (Ahrons 1994; Emery 2004; Wallerstein and Blakeslee 1989). Whether you like it or not, it's best for your children to have an ongoing relationship with both you and your ex. Since you can't get your ex out of your life completely, you might as well develop the most positive relationship you can.

Avoiding the Trickle-Down Effect

Ranked as one of the top stressors in adult life, divorce is said to bring out the worst in people. Divorce often brings a series of big changes, including moving, adjusting to a new neighborhood and changed schedules, suffering a loss of income, or all of these things. When compared to children from intact families, children in adversarial divorces are at greater risk of experiencing a whole host of future psychological problems: depression, substance abuse, and school failure (Wallerstein, Lewis, and Blakeslee 2000; Wallerstein and Blakeslee 2003). Being locked into a hostile or alienated relationship with your ex is arguably the worst stressor for your children.

Children absorb parental stress. Being mindful of this trickle-down effect will help you minimize the stress of your divorce on your children. When parents divorce, children are faced with multiple changes and challenges. In addition to possibly having to move, change schools, and make new friends, children often develop acute radar regarding the stability of their environments, especially how dependable their parents will be for them.

Children Benefit When Parents Cooperate

Arguably the number one predictor of how children of divorced parents will fare emotionally and psychologically is the degree to which their parents can cooperate and communicate (Blau 1993). Many states mandate that divorcing parents take a "parenting apart" class to learn basic skills to help their children best survive divorce. Paramount among these skills is avoiding making negative comments about the other parent and avoiding using the child as a "messenger" between parents. Befriending your ex is an extension of the cooperative parenting that most mental health professionals advise is in the best interest of the children.

Even if you were in a high-conflict marriage, the odds are that if you work at it, you will be able to get along as parents because, regardless of your differences and whether your ex engages in behavior that you consider to be "wrong," she can still be a parenting partner to you and an effective parent to your children.

Your ex may be a good-enough parent even if he was not a good-enough spouse. Your ex may be willing to collaborate with you on the child-rearing issues that arise today, tomorrow, and in the years to come. Over and over I have seen that when two former partners can cooperate around the children, over time they forge a friendship that's good for not only the children but also themselves. You may be able to access feelings of kindness, compassion, and gratitude for the person who is still your parenting partner.

For Your Own Well-Being

Life is precarious, and having enduring connections with others helps all of us feel more grounded and secure. Even if, right now, you are still soothing the wounds of your divorce, your ex might be able to be a compassionate co-parent and a generous collaborator. Hopefully, your ex is someone whom you once loved and who once loved you. Your ex is someone with whom you share a history, someone who may well represent one of the most enduring relationships of your life. There's no guarantee that you will re-couple, remarry, or stay remarried, but if you have children, you ex will forever be their parent and thus be in your life forever. You don't want to worry about a continuing negative relationship with the person with whom you are likely to share many extraordinary moments in your children's lives, from graduations and marriages to grandparenthood. Remaining enemies with your ex is bad for your mental and physical health. On the other hand, the effort you put into befriending your ex can only add value to your life.

When You Should Not Try to Befriend Your Ex

Befriending your ex isn't appropriate for everyone. If your ex-spouse is physically or emotionally abusive, or neglectful to you or your children, you may need to create space rather than connection. Substance abuse is another situation that mitigates befriending or at least requires careful evaluation.

The situation is trickier when these unacceptable behaviors occurred in the past but your ex now claims to have changed—that is, stopped abusing. In this case, consider:

- Has your ex expressed genuine remorse?

- Has your ex begun treatment, and if so, do you see these behaviors changing?

- Does your ex agree that it's crucial that these behaviors be stopped?

If you answered yes to these questions, consider letting go of the past. If, however, you answered no, befriending may not be an appropriate option right now, and further changes and communication may be necessary before you can consider it.

Befriending is not an option if your ex is emotionally inaccessible or unavailable. Not everyone can heal the wounds of divorce through reading a book like this, and if signs of grief, depression, or anxiety persist for you, seek professional assistance.

What Gets in the Way of Befriending

Even when both of you have the best of intentions, roadblocks may emerge that make you stumble in your befriending process. I've found that these roadblocks fit into one of two categories: unrealistic beliefs and strong emotions.

Unrealistic Beliefs

Unrealistic beliefs about the kind of relationship we are "supposed" to have when we divorce surround us in the images found in popular culture and society. To overcome unrealistic beliefs, first examine your belief system, and second, let go of or revise any ways of thinking that are not useful, that are dysfunctional, and that may be getting in the way of befriending your ex. Here are three common unrealistic beliefs.

My children are forever damaged by this divorce, and I am guilty. Early research on the effects of divorce on children dealt a devastating blow to divorcing parents. In a series of impressive longitudinal studies, Judith Wallerstein and her colleagues (Wallerstein and Blakeslee 1989, 2003; Wallerstein, Lewis, and Blakeslee 2000) warned parents that divorce is a "cumulative trauma" from which children never fully recover. Their research encourages parents to think long and hard before divorcing, and gave rise to a generation of guilty divorcing parents. Although subsequent research challenges these dire conclusions (Ahrons 1994; Emery 2004; Hetherington and Kelly 2002) and emphasizes that collaborative parenting can assuage the damaging impact of divorce, it's easy to see that guilt-ridden parents might shy away from befriending one another, since remaining "enemies" may seem to justify the divorce. Too often I have heard a befriended relationship spurned or dismissed with this type of comment: "If they were able to be friends, why didn't they simply stay married?"

I'm done with my ex. A friend relayed that at one point during her divorce proceedings, her attorney had said, "You don't want this jerk in your life forever!" Unfortunately, this belief is deeply ingrained in what I call the "culture of divorce." In one way, the lawyer was correct: my friend didn't want "this jerk" in her life forever. But because small children were involved, my friend did want their father involved in their lives and, by extension, in her life as well. Believing that an ex will always be a jerk (rather than a person who acted like a jerk during a difficult period) is a negative, self-defeating belief that gets in the way of befriending. Because my friend was able to see, over time, that her ex behaved reasonably and well toward their children—and no longer acted like a jerk—the two were able to eventually befriend one another. She's not done with her ex, and that's a positive thing. He is possibly in her life forever (and her attorney isn't).

Getting even is the best revenge. I know of nothing worse for all parties concerned than divorce-court proceedings that drag on for years, sometimes decades, because one or both spouses want to "get even." Everyone loses in these scenarios. Astronomical amounts of money, time, and energy are spent that could be allocated differently. The person who "wins" a custody suit has to live with having made her child's other parent (and very possibly the child as well) deeply angry in ways that harm the child. Winning a hefty financial settlement by bankrupting your ex means you'll have to live with the fact that your child must now visit your ex in compromised financial circumstances.

Nor is getting even in smaller ways of much help to the fragile process of befriending. If your ex sends the children to your house with unwashed clothes, you need not repay him in kind. His returning the children later than expected is no reason for you to repeat that behavior when you return them to him. Befriending means letting go of revenge.

Difficult Emotions

It's easy to harbor animosity toward your ex, who has undoubtedly hurt or angered you. Grief, anger, anxiety, resentment, guilt, and jealousy are some of the feelings you may have faced already if you have divorced or are getting divorced.

This book encourages you to embrace your emotions, regardless of how difficult it is to deal with them. However, that's *not* the same as having a license to act them out. In fact, the opposite is true: learning to feel, accept, and manage your emotions allows you to feel safer about embracing them if only because you won't fear being overcome by them. I've developed a five-step process for dealing with difficult emotions that you will learn more about in the next chapter and have a chance to practice throughout this book:

1. Recognize when you are feeling a difficult emotion.

2. Breathe into your emotions to calm down.

3. Name and befriend your emotions.

4. Accept your emotions.

5. Communicate effectively.

Throughout this book I'll use and expand this model in specific ways so that your difficult emotions don't interfere with befriending your ex. Here are some of the most difficult emotions you are likely to encounter in the process of befriending your ex.

Grief

Divorce always involves loss. Sadness and grief are inevitable in the aftermath of divorce, and the capacity to process these feelings is crucial to a healthy adjustment. (Chapter 3 details how the grief process unfolds.) Many people, after the initial upheaval of divorce, are able to activate their own inner resources and adequately adjust. The important thing to remember is that allowing yourself to mourn your losses is essential to moving forward into a productive life, one that includes a new relationship with a befriended ex. Unresolved grief, on the other hand, can get in your way and prevent you from having a positive relationship with your ex.

Anger

Rarely have I witnessed a divorce that doesn't involve anger and resentment. But holding on to grudges and negative feelings does no one any good, least of all you. Recent research (Goleman 1995, 2006) has documented the high cost of anger, which releases high levels of adrenaline and cortisol and wears us down. Although often understandable and inevitable at some points during the divorce process, unrelenting anger is not only harmful to your health but also an impediment to an amicable postdivorce relationship with your ex. Will your ex be magically transformed into a person who always parents the children as you would like? Probably not. She may allow them to eat more junk food when they are with her than seems healthy. She may not be as attentive to their homework as appears necessary for academic success. She may date your former coworker or take a vacation you know she can't afford. But these are not good reasons to blow up at your ex. That would only feed animosity when you are aiming for positive feelings. The truth is that anger ties you to an unhealthy relationship, perhaps the very one you had when you were unhappily married. Chapter 4 discusses productive ways to handle your anger, but the short answer is that you eventually have to let go of your anger if you want a fulfilling postdivorce relationship with your ex.

Anxiety

Building a new, postdivorce life always involves anxiety. You are facing the world now as a single person rather than as part of a couple, and that can be scary. If something goes wrong, you have only yourself to blame. There's no one to remind you to pay the water bill or go to the doctor for that nagging cough. Perhaps your ex did the taxes, or did most of the driving or all of the grocery shopping. You will have to learn new skills and master tasks for which your ex once took responsibility. All these feelings are natural and expected. The danger is if your anxieties overwhelm you to the point where you can't take any of the risks that living solo entails. You want to make sure that your anxiety about your ex's past behavior or life in general doesn't prevent you from stepping into the new, and perhaps uncomfortable, place of befriending your ex and enjoying a beneficial relationship.

Guilt

Guilt may arise as a result of the awareness that one partner is inflicting pain on the other or their children. Parents have an understandable sense of responsibility over bringing hardship into their children's lives. A parent whose marriage fails is likely to think, *I made a mistake.* Guilt over bringing discomfort to your children is a normal response to divorce.

Guilt arises for other reasons too. Divorce has many liberating aspects. Raising children is hard work, and divorced parents get unexpected time off. Divorced parents may feel guilty about "enjoying time off" while their children suffer. When I got divorced, there was a joke about this; perhaps you've heard this story: Divorced partners Ralph and Anna run into one another at a party. Ralph says to his ex-wife, "Wow, you look terrific!" Anna replies that she feels great and has been working out five days a week. "You look healthier too," she says to Ralph, who is tanned and relaxed. Suddenly, Ralph looks at Anna and asks, "How are the kids?" "The kids?" she replies. "I thought they were with you."

We laugh because this joke belies the notion that divorce brings only misery. The truth is that divorce can be a very positive life change. It can be liberating compared to the stress of an unhappy marriage. It can allow you to focus on your well-being, and give you free time. It can benefit your children as well, by expanding their ties to extended family. At the same time, the joke's ending plays into our guilt over how divorce shortchanges children; it implies that the children have been forgotten or overlooked if both parents are out on the town and looking so good. The story highlights the parents' discomfort about the congenial nature of their interaction: they'd forgotten they were supposed to be hostile and, instead, showered one another with compliments.

Another source of guilt may be feelings about aspects of your behavior during your marriage. Feeling bad about your behavior is normal. All marriages face innumerable difficulties, and marital partners are rarely polite, nice, and generous to one another 100 percent of the time. Chances are you behaved just as badly as your ex did at times during your marriage. In moments of extreme emotion, perhaps you said things to your ex that you now regret. You may have remorse about things you did as well. It would be unusual if you didn't, at some time, feel guilty for the collateral damage wrought on the children, friends, or family members. Again, the problem arises if your guilty feelings overwhelm your capacity to befriend. It's never too late to apologize. The benefits of befriending are worth the dangers of crossing the divide between your ex and you that results from guilt.

Shame

Shame involves painful feelings of depression, alienation, inadequacy, and worthlessness. Shame is an extreme but common reaction to divorce. Many people use the words "guilt" and "shame" interchangeably, but they actually refer to different experiences. While a guilty person says, "I've done something wrong," a person who experiences shame says, "There's something wrong with me" (Bradshaw 1988). Sometimes divorce triggers both emotions. For example, at a dinner party one night, Xavier said something nasty and hurtful about his ex. Afterward, he felt guilty because he could see that he had intentionally hurt her. More painful were his feelings of shame: he also felt ashamed that he was a person who would behave so despicably.

Divorce and befriending are critical processes that push you to examine your emotional responses. In addition, they push you to reevaluate your assumptions, beliefs, and perspectives. And finally, they offer you the opportunity to stretch into unknown territory.

Creating a New Vision: Befriending

Whether you realize it or not, you are always choosing a perspective that either enriches or diminishes your reality.

The Power of Your Beliefs

In the book *What Happy People Know: How the New Science of Happiness Can Change Your Life for the Better*, psychologist Dan Baker and Cameron Stauth (2003) remind us that no matter how difficult your life is, you always have the power to rise above suffering. This idea is particularly important during divorce, since divorce always brings us face to face with new and challenging situations, events, and emotions. We bring our chosen perspectives to every new challenge; becoming mindful that we always bring our own biases or chosen perspectives to each new situation and event we face is an important step in assessing reality.

Examining Your Belief System

We tend to operate on autopilot. Here's an exercise that can help you become aware of how your autopilot manages your belief system when it comes to divorce.

Exercise 1.1 Identify Your Autopilot

Take in a deep breath, let it out, and bring to mind the images you grew up with about what "being divorced" means. Slowly review your life, scanning backward to your early childhood memories through today. Ask yourself: What did you learn about divorce in your family? Did your parents divorce? Did you have any divorced relatives or friends when you were growing up? Did you have friends with divorced parents? Did your parents socialize with people who were divorced? Were there divorced people in your neighborhood or at your school? What did you learn about divorce from books, movies, and television? What stories do you carry with you about what divorce means?

Pause, take a breath, and recall what images arose when you considered the questions. Jot down the names of any divorced people that came up during this exercise as well as your thoughts, feelings, and memories. What messages did you get from your family about "being divorced"? Think about the composite picture you hold from the images evoked. See if you can find a word or phrase that sums up your impression of "being divorced," and jot it in your journal.

Here are some of my clients' responses:

- Janey became aware that her impressions were all filled with negative images of "broken families" and lonely, unmarried women.

- Haily realized that her family admired and revered her divorced Aunt Daisy, a belle-of-the-ball type.

- John's images of divorce focused on his father, who had abandoned him. He realized that he feared that divorce would doom him to follow in his father's footsteps.

- Ron realized that his image of divorce was of a happy playboy.

Very few people have internalized an image of a positive divorce, where ex-spouses befriend one another. Without a positive vision or model of what an ex-spouse can be like, it's understandable that so many of us carry around debilitating stereotypes and have trouble creating something workable.

Now, take a deep breath. Notice how you are responding to the previous statement. Think about what it would mean for you to develop an excellent working relationship with your former spouse. In your journal, jot down three specific ideas or behaviors that a befriended relationship would entail.

If you had trouble with the previous exercise, consider these snapshots of how befriending can look:

Jane was divorced for two years when hurricane toppled several trees in her yard. Her driveway was strewn with branches. She called her ex Richie, a contractor, and asked if he would ask one of his workers to come to her house first thing in the morning to remove the debris so she could get to work on time. The next morning, when her driveway was cleared out, she tried to pay the worker for the job, but he said, "Don't worry. Richie took care of this for you." Jane told me, "Even though we're no longer married, Richie still wants to take care of me and the girls. And you know what? I think he likes doing it, and so do I."

Sara and Johnnie had split up twenty-five years ago from a decades-long relationship, when they found themselves sitting in the waiting room of the local hospital, each with a dying mother. Sara's mother died first and then Johnnie's. Sara and Johnnie comforted one another after their losses. After the funerals and burials, when all the out-of-town relatives had left, Johnnie wrote to Sara: "Thank you for caring about me now and throughout this terrible part of my life. You will always be important to me and an important part of my family."

Exercise 1.2 Expand Your Belief System

Take a few deep breaths and recall how you felt in your body as you read the previous vignettes. Did you feel a softening or opening, or perhaps a tightness? Our bodies give us important emotional information. Is your body signaling you with a positive response or with fear? What messages does your body give you in response to these stories? Notice how you react to the idea that exes can support one another, and record your feelings in your journal.

The hormone *oxytocin* is released when we experience and witness caring behavior, and it may deepen our ability to bond with others. Hearing stories about generous, compassionate, and considerate exes can open you to unexpressed feelings and hidden yearnings. Now note in your journal any new ideas about how you want your divorce to unfold.

In my office, I have found that exes often feel uncomfortable or even ashamed to admit to having caring feelings for an ex-spouse, as if a taboo forbade feeling compassion and care—and even love—for the divorced partner.

Translating Your Ideas into Action

Take a moment to consider the current state of your relationship with your ex. You may be reading this book without knowing what you ultimately want in terms of a relationship with your ex. However, you probably have immediate concerns and are pondering what you need to do to create a friendlier relationship. Here's a critical question that can help you think concretely, positively, and practically: *Is there one small step I might take that could create an opening to a new relationship with my ex?*

Exercise 1.3 Three Steps to Begin Befriending

My three-step model can help you begin to translate your desires into a new reality:

1. Assess your current relationship with your ex; write down three strengths and three liabilities.

2. How would a more befriended relationship with your ex look? Jot down some ideas, or write a paragraph or two.

3. Imagine taking one small step toward befriending your ex. What would that step be? Write it down.

• Every Journey Begins with One Small Step: Jeb's Story

This three-step model helped Jeb, a shy thirty-seven-year-old man, create a befriended relationship with Kim, his ex. Jeb joined a therapy group and expressed dissatisfaction with his custody arrangement. Although he wanted to spend more time with his children, he was reluctant to talk to Kim, afraid to upset what was essentially a distant but conflict-free relationship. As he discussed his reluctance, he became aware of an internal roadblock: guilt. He admitted he hadn't shouldered his responsibility when the children were babies, hadn't paid his dues by getting up at night or changing diapers. This had been a conflict between Jeb and Kim throughout their marriage. And that guilt made him feel that he now had no right to tell Kim he wanted to spend more time with the children. But as he spoke in the group, he remembered working full-time when the children were small, while Kim had been a stay-at-home mother. So, with the help of the group, he began absorbing the idea that he might not have been such a bad father after all!

With group support, Jeb finally took what was, for him, a big step and requested a meeting with Kim. He began by apologizing for past behavior he now recognized must have been difficult for Kim. He complimented his ex-wife on her strengths, especially her parenting skills. To his surprise, Kim was open. She was flattered by his compliments and willing to negotiate. He was amazed that simply apologizing and stating his regret made Kim willing to accommodate his desire for more frequent visitation.

Communication between the two improved. Shortly after this interchange, Kim asked for a few changes in their drop-off and pickup schedule. She began talking about how imbalanced their relationship was and how overburdened she felt. Within a year they had created a new ritual: each August they would examine their custody arrangement, and assess how their and their children's needs were being met in the current situation. Recognizing his feelings, apologizing, and taking the risk of asking for what he needed helped Jeb with his befriending journey.

Conclusion

Regardless of where you are now in your relationship with your ex—alienated, hostile, hurt, sneering, neutral, cordial, and so on—you can work toward befriending. You've learned how society perpetuates the myth of the bad divorce, damaging you, your kids, and, yes, your ex.

The next chapter introduces you to the core befriending skills and essential mind-sets that will help you create a better relationship. Remember, a befriended ex is one of the secrets to a divorced person's happiness.

CHAPTER 2

core befriending skills

Carla sat in my office, weeping: "You are asking me to control my emotions and my big mouth, and think about the big picture? If I could have done that, I probably wouldn't be getting divorced!" Like Carla, you may let too much hang out. Or you may keep too much in, only to explode later. You may wonder whether it's really possible to befriend your ex given all the challenges involved. Yes! It's very possible, but it will take an open mind and some hard work on your part.

In this chapter I identify two core skills and two core mind-sets that form the basis of befriending your ex. Although neither the skills nor mind-sets are complicated, you will probably reread this chapter several times before finishing this book, because retraining ourselves isn't simple.

At the basis of managing your emotions is developing *mindfulness skills*, which will give you the opportunity for enormous growth. You will become a more aware person, which will help you not only in the process of befriending your ex, but also in all of your current and future relationships. At the core of befriending your ex is learning to manage your own difficult emotions, a skill addressed with an array of strategies and suggestions.

As part of dealing with difficult emotions, this chapter will also introduce you to the value of journal writing, which will help you weather the emotionally rough waters that can accompany the befriending process. You can use either a traditional journal that you purchase or the companion journal, which you can access at judithruskayrabinorphd .com/companionjournal.

As mentioned, there are also two crucial mind-sets to keep in the forefront of your mind when things get tough with your ex. The first is to *keep the big picture in mind*, which means living and making decisions with your children's needs in mind first. It means prioritizing your children and protecting them from emotional harm, and maximizing their chances for well-being.

The second crucial mind-set is to *take the high road*, which means to always—or at least whenever you can muster it—act in accordance with your "self at best" (Fosha 2000), your highest and most compassionate self. It means bringing kindness and generosity to every member of your family, including your ex. Basically, divorcing parents need to always remember to "love their kids more than they hate their ex" (Emery 2004, 291).

When you are able to access both the skills and the mind-sets, befriending will eventually require less effort.

Developing Mindfulness Skills

Mindfulness is a powerful tool that will help you meet the emotional challenges that invariably arise in developing a new relationship with your ex. This section explains what mindfulness is and helps you begin practicing it.

The simplest definition of *mindfulness* is being aware of the present moment. Mindfulness entails intentionally cultivating awareness of what is. To be mindful is to stop and notice your thoughts and feelings in the present moment. Mindfulness helps us accept painful thoughts and feelings without struggling against them and trying to change them. Mindfulness is simply becoming aware; it's a mind-set and a discipline you can develop while standing in line at the grocery store, walking, exercising, driving, cooking, or even working.

Helping you develop a regular mindfulness practice is beyond the scope of this book. (For a more complete introduction to mindfulness, see *Mindfulness for Beginners* by Jon Kabat-Zinn or *Mindsight* by Daniel Siegel.) However, practicing the exercises in this book can help you become more aware of and sensitive to your internal experiences. Remaining mindful will greatly help you make conscious and mindful (rather than impulsive and mindless) decisions concerning your postdivorce relationship with your ex.

Mindfulness comprises several components, all of which become more habitual with practice:

- Being in touch with the present moment as opposed to being caught up in thoughts about the past (rumination) or future (worry). When you find yourself ruminating or worrying, perhaps tell yourself: *Stop.*

- Learning to focus your attention on one thing at a time. This includes things going on around you (sights and sounds) and things going on inside you (thoughts and feelings).

- Having a nonjudgmental attitude. This includes observing inner and outer experiences objectively, as opposed to labeling them as either "good" or "bad." An important part of this skill is self-compassion. When we have compassion for ourselves, even when we feel an emotion we might normally judge as "bad," we can let go of the judgment and simply experience the emotion.

- Observing things as they truly are, as opposed to having preconceived notions or being on autopilot.

One of the simplest ways to experience mindfulness is to focus on your breathing. The following exercise allows you to be mindful right now. Read the exercise slowly as you follow the instructions.

Exercise 2.1 Mindful Breathing

Find a quiet space and sit down. Get comfortable and allow yourself to relax. Take three or four deep breaths, breathing in through your nose and out through your mouth, letting the exhalation last a bit longer than the inhalation. Inhale and exhale, inhale and exhale—in and out—and inhale and exhale. There's nowhere to go, nothing to do; just breathe. Now, become aware of your body. Notice how your body connects: how your bottom makes contact with the seat of your chair; notice your feet on the floor, your hands on your lap or the arm of your chair. Be aware of your own breathing rhythm. Inhaling deeply and fully, imagine that you are taking the air from deep within the earth, and then let it go. Inhale and release, inhale and release. Let the air fill your body and then let it go, exhaling. Let the inhalation and exhalation be gentle and smooth; be aware of the sensations in your body, and if your mind wanders, gently return it to your breathing.

Take a moment to notice what it's like for you to slow down and be with your experience. Now, take out your journal and reflect on your experience through writing about it.

A Note on Breathing

Throughout this book are many opportunities to practice mindfulness exercises, many of which include breathing. Be sure to breathe from your belly rather than your chest, and breathe in through your nose and out through your mouth. Remember, whenever you are upset, focusing on the sound and rhythm of your breath can calm you down and help you feel grounded in the present moment, which helps you manage your emotions.

Dealing with Difficult Emotions

Experiencing difficult emotions during divorce and its aftermath is the norm. Grief, anger, guilt, shame, anxiety, and other uncomfortable feelings can interfere with befriending. Pushing away difficult emotions won't help. Becoming controlled by them won't either. Actively dealing with your difficult emotions, through the exercises outlined next and by using your journal, is key to befriending first yourself and then your ex.

A Five-Step Process for Dealing with Difficult Emotions

What follows is a five-step process for dealing with difficult emotions like grief, anger, resentment, guilt, shame, anxiety, and other feelings that interfere with befriending. These steps help you identify, use, understand, and manage your emotions constructively. Practicing the exercises will help you develop specific skills. Although the skills are meant for use in the moment that you start noticing your angry feelings becoming activated, I recommend practicing them whenever you can.

Think of these exercises as an "emotional workout," similar to the one you do to get your body physically fit, except that now you're working on strengthening your ability to manage your emotions. Each time you practice any of the steps, you're developing your capacity to manage your distress and gain control over painful feelings and behaviors. Remember, the goal is not to eliminate difficult emotions—because that's impossible. The goal is to slow down enough to think about what your emotions or thoughts are teaching you, and to respond from a calm, centered place.

Step 1: Recognize When You Are Feeling a Difficult Emotion

Difficult emotions can be threatening. Here are three common reactions to a perceived threat; some people exhibit one of these patterns, while others exhibit all:

- *Fight:* Getting aggressive and agitated

- *Flight:* Removing yourself as quickly as possible, avoiding the situation

- *Freeze:* Shutting down, spacing out, being immobilized

Exercise 2.2 Identify Your Threat Response

Take a moment to bring to mind one or two times when you experienced a difficult emotion, such as anger, resentment, jealousy, or hurt, during your relationship with your ex. Reflect on your reactions: did you fight, flee, or freeze, or did you react in a combination of these ways? All of us have an emotional style, an emotional blueprint. You may be the kind of person people describe as "over the top" (you express your feelings emphatically) or "cool as a cucumber." What's your emotional style? Jot down your response in your journal.

Step 2: Breathe into Your Emotions to Calm Down

Deep breathing is such an important, helpful, and easily accessible skill for calming your nervous system that there are reminders about it throughout this book. The important thing is to recognize that our bodies can be tools for self-calming. We live in a culture that overvalues the mind and often teaches us to "figure out" why we are upset. Many people are unaware that we can calm down simply by calming our bodies. The key here is that when we calm the body, we calm the mind.

Think about a situation you identified in the previous step. As you hold the situation and your response in mind, breathe deeply. Perhaps review exercise 2.1 to master deep breathing. Notice what you feel in your body and whether your response changes as you breathe slowly and deeply. Write in your journal what it's like to practice deep breathing to calm down.

I suggest using this technique on a regular basis. It's important to practice in nonemotional moments, such as when you get up in the morning or get into bed at night. Practice when situations arise with your ex and in other areas of your life.

Step 3: Name and Befriend Your Emotions

Naming your emotions is another calming technique. Often the simple act of "naming" something disempowers it. Read the following list, noticing how you feel when you name these emotions. Notice whether you embrace or push away these emotions, and jot down your responses in your journal.

anger	anxiety	depression
fear	grief	guilt
jealousy	sadness	worry

Now, review the list and recall a time when you felt each emotion in your relationship with your ex. Take a moment to just be with your memory and the feelings evoked. Allow yourself to locate your feelings in your body. Write about how you feel, and recognize your own emotional style. Whenever you feel upset, agitated, anxious, or uncomfortable, simply naming your feelings can help you calm down. If you aren't sure exactly what you are feeling, it's perfectly okay to recognize just that, and to know that you are overwhelmed and unsure of what you feel. Take a deep breath and just sit with this new awareness, and see if you notice a shift in your body.

Step 4: Accept Your Emotions

Feeling your feelings is fine! Accepting all your feelings, even your confusing ones, is fine. But feelings do not give you permission to act hurtfully. It's important to be able to sit with your feelings, locate them in your body, and breathe. Over time, doing so enables you to access a window of opportunity that gives you that split second within which you can respond rather than react!

Exercise 2.3 Breathe into Your Emotions without Acting on Them

In the previous exercise, you made a list of specific situations and emotions that triggered your unhealthy behaviors. Pick one of the situations or emotions, and take a moment to recall how you felt then. You may notice yourself getting upset all over again, but this is okay. Breathe, and identify where in your body this feeling lives. Mindfully track any tension in your body as you name your emotion. Give yourself permission to feel and name your feelings. Consciously decide *not* to make any decisions or take any immediate action, knowing that you can plan what to do when you calm down.

You will benefit from practicing deep breathing regularly, especially when you aren't upset. To practice, simply recall an upsetting event in order to trigger your emotions. Remember, each time you practice any of the exercises in this book, you're strengthening a new "muscle."

Step 5: Communicate Effectively

Take a moment to remember the last time you and your ex had an upsetting conversation. As you recall the conversation, what do you think or feel about your part in it? Can you imagine how this conversation might have flowed and what might have transpired if you'd calmed down? Although we can't change others' behavior, we do have control over our own. If you could redo that conversation from a calmer place, how could you make it less antagonistic, more satisfactory?

The following are some suggestions for how to communicate effectively once you've calmed down.

Stay focused in the present. Focus on the issue at hand, rather than going off on tangents. Even if your ex tries to change the subject or raise other issues, you can stay focused on what you want to achieve if you remain mindful and calm. If you expect a conversation to be upsetting, consider writing down your goals for the conversation before getting into it, including what questions you want answered and what decisions you want to make. Mindfully selecting the words you use will steer the conversation away from confrontation. As you speak, keep your list in front of you to remind you of your goals and the topic at hand.

Avoid bringing up the past. You and your ex are in the process of forming a new relationship. Keep that thought in the front of your mind. You are no longer married, and the expectations and goals you once shared are no longer relevant—nor are your previous controversies. What's important now is focusing on the present goals and interactions. Even if your ex was nasty or childish in the past, try to segregate that part of your life from the present. Make it your conscious intention not to bring it up during current negotiations.

Be mindful of nonverbal communication cues. This includes your tone of voice, as well as the timing and pacing of your speech. My father used to tell me, "It's not what you say, but the way you say it, that counts." Later, when I was in psychotherapy training, I heard the same concept: "A good therapist can say anything to anyone." The words we use are often not as important as the messages communicated by our facial expressions, our tone of voice, and even how we hold our bodies.

Cultivate a gentle tone of voice. Keep in mind that the look in your eye and your tone of voice are as important as your words. Practice accessing the compassionate part of yourself. Recall a time when you were kind to a loved one. Doing so helps you realize how you feel when you cultivate kindness. Remember, kindness helps all of us! Your ex's request to change who has the kids for a weekend is not life threatening.

Use "I" statements. Express how *you* feel, rather than begin sentences with "you," which is blaming.

Don't say everything. Saying everything, without regard for how it might make the other person feel, inevitably gets us in trouble. Practice politeness (see chapter 6).

Practice letting go. Holding on to hurt, resentment, and anger damages your relationships, your health, and your state of mind and interferes with befriending.

Have important conversations in person or by phone, not via e-mail.
Although e-mail is a wonderful tool for keeping track of arrangements
and schedules, be mindful of its limitations. First, people often e-mail
precisely because they don't really want to communicate face to face or
voice to voice; they simply want to "leave a message." Second, e-mail
messages are easily subject to misinterpretation. Face-to-face conversation and even phone messages provide us with voice and body language
cues that e-mail lacks, and they offer a better pathway for genuine emotions to be communicated with less risk of misinterpretation.

Remember, if you aren't sure what you want to say, use your journal
to clarify your own emotions so that you can either communicate better
or choose not to communicate at all. Write what you feel.

Journal Writing

While solid communication skills are at the core of befriending,
sometimes when you are distressed, trying to talk can backfire. Journal
writing is an incredibly powerful tool that can help you calm down and
meet the emotional challenges involved in befriending your ex. This tool
is useful for recording your process and progress with using mindfulness
and managing your emotions (Pennebaker 1997).

In her widely read and moving journal, Anne Frank (1995, 6) wrote
that "paper has more patience than people," highlighting the importance
of writing as a tool for self-reflection. Writing helps us listen to our feelings. Using your journal will help you embrace your thoughts and feelings
rather than act out. Author Virginia Woolf confessed (1976, 75) that in
putting a painful experience into words, she could "make it whole" and
that "this wholeness means it has lost its power to hurt [her]," again tes-
tifying to the power of the written word to help us work through difficult
experiences. Writing has been useful to many of my clients. If you make
time to do the exercises in this book, you will reap the benefits. Here are
some specific suggestions to help you use your writing more effectively:

- Find a location where there will be no disturbances from
  others.

- Write continuously, without regard for spelling or grammar.

- Remember: the writing is for you, and only you.

- Write about what matters to you, your deepest thoughts and feelings.

- Don't avoid the painful parts—and don't forget the good stuff!

- Set aside time to write as often as possible, ideally every day.

Managing Your Mind-Sets

Managing your mind-sets—your assumptions and beliefs—is crucial to befriending. An example of the power of mind-set comes from athletic competition: athletes in training for various competitions emphasize the importance of imagination. Simply imagining success leads to success! While skills are important, your attitude is crucial. If you are constantly cursing, ruminating, or *catastrophizing* (imagining the worst), mindfulness and journal writing won't be enough to help the befriending process unfold. Much like other skills, having a particular mind-set can be learned and developed until it becomes habitual.

Befriending Mind-Set 1: Keep the Big Picture in Mind

If you truly want to live in accordance with the research findings (Ahrons 1994) that children benefit most when divorced parents get along, then this is the "big picture" that you must keep in mind. When you find yourself losing steam, remind yourself that befriending your ex benefits your children. Here's an exercise that can help.

Exercise 2.4 Sticky-Note Reminder to Imagine Success

The daughter of one of my divorced clients was about to graduate from high school. My client worried about how graduation day would go, because her ex and his new girlfriend would also be there. She wrote "Lily's graduation" on a sticky note and told me that whenever she saw it, she deliberately and consciously imagined seeing her daughter's smiling face as she wore the traditional cap and gown. My client placed the sticky note on her bathroom mirror as a reminder to "be a family" at the graduation ceremony, even if it meant she would have to set aside past hurts and resentments, and to be friendly to her ex and his girlfriend. After the graduation ceremony, she texted me, "The sticky note worked! We did just great!"

Try to find an image that reminds you of the value of befriending. Now see if you can find the words that go with the image. Remind yourself of why you want to befriend your ex. Write whatever words come to mind on a sticky note and place it on your mirror, or the refrigerator, or someplace else where you will see this reminder often.

Befriending Mind-Set 2: Take the High Road

Every day, on the news we hear about the atrocious ways that people are cruel to one another. Taking the high road is about adding kindness to your small corner of the world. You can choose to squabble and seek revenge, or you can develop the mind-set of taking the high road, which includes choosing to focus on the positives in others and ignoring their limitations. You can consciously decide to be considerate and generous to your ex. Small moments of empathy and compassion that make life sweeter for your ex may well have a ripple effect, influencing your ex's attitude and treatment of you.

Developing Compassion for Your Ex

It's crucial to simply acknowledge that your ex may be in pain. It's easy to forget that he may be hurting, and to see him as a monster. But remember: we are all human beings who crave attention, recognition, affection, and love. The following technique, which has helped my clients connect to their compassion for their exes, may be helpful to you.

Exercise 2.5: Practice Developing Compassion

Jot down your responses to these three questions in your journal:

1. What personal qualities did you most admire about your ex when you first met?

2. What do you see as your ex's greatest strengths now?

3. What do you see as your ex's greatest resources?

There's a deliberate strategy to this line of questioning. These questions cultivate compassion and aim to connect you to your natural kindness. They may connect you to a warm, soft place within, where compassion lives. Remember to ask yourself these questions whenever you feel fed up or burned out.

Here's one example of how these questions have helped my clients access lost memories that sparked their compassion: twenty years after her divorce, a client of mine recalled how touched she was when her ex had ordered an extra, enlarged school picture of their daughter for her.

Even when reciprocity doesn't occur, we grow when we express compassion to others. It's never too late to make a peace offering.

Exercise 2.6 Offer an Olive Branch

In biblical days, giving someone an olive branch symbolized a peace offering. What if your ex brings the children home a bit late? Take a moment to imagine handing her an olive branch. Or, imagine sweetly saying, "Forget it! Let's take a time-out!" What kind of feelings come up as you imagine consciously de-escalating hurt feelings between you and your ex?

On a scale from 1 to 10 (where 1 means "uncomfortable" and 10 means "very comfortable"), how comfortable are you with this image? Write down "olive branch" or "time-out" in your journal and the number that represents how comfortable you feel about making a peace offering.

We will return to this idea of offering an olive branch when we discuss forgiveness in chapter 6. When in doubt about how to handle a particular situation, remember to take the high road.

Embracing a New Vision: Befriending

As I have already stated, our expectations and attitudes are crucial in shaping our reality. This concept is so important that it bears repeating. We all have conscious and unconscious notions, expectations, and visions of life. Our expectations are crucial: they shape how we interpret what happens. For example, a rainy day may mean one thing to you if you are planning to play tennis, and another if you are looking forward to curling up in your pajamas with a good book.

Social expectations and attitudes differ around the world. In some countries, women are not expected to drive a car, and a woman who does is considered, at the very least, improper. In developed countries, however, teenage girls learn to drive at the same time as their male peers do, and it's expected that women and men will share a gender-neutral road through life. What this means is that the expectations and attitudes you hold about divorce and the relationship between ex-spouses hugely influences the experience you create. Befriending your ex hasn't gotten as much press as remaining enemies.

In reading this book, you are choosing to explore a cultural shift. As you read on, embrace any ideas or behaviors that speak to you, and leave behind those that don't. Remember, you have the right to be flexible and creative in designing your befriended relationship. Keep your heart and mind open.

The Wolf of Love and Compassion

Carla, whom you met at the beginning of this chapter, sat in my office expressing remorse. The previous evening, she'd "lost it" and been nasty to Barry, her ex, when he, once again, brought the children home late. "We'd agreed how important it is to make the switching hour calm and peaceful, but there I went and lost my patience. I was probably also angry about his new girlfriend, but that's no excuse: I should know that Barry's lateness isn't intentional spitefulness or meanness—he was late our entire marriage! But I truly blasted him," she said regretfully. "What a mess! I know he felt horrible when the children got upset—and so did I."

I reminded Carla that a goal of being mindful and containing her negative feelings 100 percent of the time was unrealistic. To emphasize the importance of self-compassion and compassion for her ex, I told her a story from Rick Hanson (2009, 121–132), author of *Buddha's Brain: The Practical Neuroscience of Happiness, Love, and Wisdom*:

> An aging Native American grandmother was on her deathbed.
> Her granddaughter asked what she had done to become so
> wise, loved, and respected. The dying woman replied, "I always
> try to remember there are two wolves in my heart, a wolf of
> love and a wolf of hate. And I know that everything depends
> on which one I feed each day."

All of us have a wolf of love and a wolf of hate, and when we become judgmental, irritable, nasty, and argumentative, the wolf of hate has taken over.

Carla admitted that whenever the wolf of hate took her over and she was mean to Barry, she felt ashamed of herself. I asked her to do an exercise with me. I led her through a visualization in which she saw herself waiting for her children. Then I asked her if she could feel compassion for her worry and sadness. Her eyes filled with tears. "And can you bring that compassion to Barry?" I asked. Carla looked away, and I wasn't sure if my intervention had had the intended impact. I reminded her that when the wolf of hate is activated, our cortisol levels and stress rise, and when the wolf of love is activated, we stimulate the production of oxytocin, the love hormone, and generally feel better about ourselves.

In the next session, I was delighted to hear that Carla had apologized to Barry for blowing up. She felt that their glitch was now repaired, which reminds me:

- The path to the high road begins with self-compassion.

- Forgiving yourself is often a prelude to asking your ex for forgiveness.

- Children do best when their parents behave civilly and respectfully toward one another.

Conclusion

In this chapter you've learned the basic skills and mind-sets of befriending. You can see how mindful awareness is at the core of managing your emotions and at the basis of maintaining the two befriending mind-sets. Again and again you will return to mindfulness and mindful breathing as keys to mastering letting go, forgiving, developing compassion, and other skills necessary for befriending your ex. You may want to return to the five-step process for dealing with difficult emotions introduced in this chapter. Reminding yourself of your mind-sets, using the questions for developing compassion, and offering an olive branch are all strategies that can help you when you feel disheartened.

The next chapter focuses in greater depth on one of the most difficult emotions evoked in the befriending process: grief. Although many of us wish we could avoid the unpleasant feelings of grief, sadness, and loss, they are an inevitable and necessary part of the befriending journey that unfolds differently for each of us.

CHAPTER 3

grief as a pathway to resiliency

Divorce is one of the greatest losses we can experience. As a stressful experience, it's right up there with death of a friend or loved one, job loss, and moving. Even when it's for the best, divorce involves the loss of routines, stability, and relationships that provide us with solid anchors in a complicated world filled with adversity. Divorce sounds the death knell of a marriage, the end of a shared vision of a certain kind of life together. It's the loss of the simplicity of an intact family. If there are children involved, you will see on their faces and in their behaviors the sadness you may have brought into their lives. Often, as in the following examples, it's the small loss that allows us to tap into grief:

> Essie, a twenty-year-old office manager who was separated from her husband, found that something as seemingly mundane as getting a new telephone number and informing everyone that she could no longer be reached at her old number made her inexplicably burst into sobbing.

> Eduardo felt helpless and angry whenever he couldn't find the measuring cup, the scissors, the extra blankets; he felt lost at the realization that his ex-wife had organized the house and that, once she had left, he couldn't find the things that made his life easier.

Joan and her husband, who lived in New England, separated in the spring. Not until six months later, in the middle of a heavy snowstorm, did Joan realize how frightened she was to drive in the snow. She grieved anew for the partner she had lost, one who was adept at driving in the snow. Sometimes when we are unwilling to recognize the loss of a person, we are able to recognize the loss of that person's function.

Do you recognize yourself in any of the previous examples? Grief doesn't always travel in a straight line: it can pop up unexpectedly, even long after we have experienced a loss, or it can be expressed in other ways, such as anger.

Unfortunately, many people avoid and even resist grieving a divorce. That's not surprising, given that our culture has few rituals to help with grieving the end of a marriage. When there's a death, the relatives of the deceased usually gather to perform traditional funeral rituals and to give one another emotional support. But our society doesn't yet have traditional rituals to help those affected by the death of a marriage.

The Purpose of Grief

A universal finding from diverse psychological and spiritual theories is that unresolved grief has far-reaching effects, often resulting in chronic emotional and physical problems (Worden 2009). Making time to *actively* grieve is crucial for your well-being now and in the future. I emphasize the word "actively" because grief is not a passive process. It requires conscious effort and determination. Especially if you are interested in cultivating a better relationship with your ex, you will need to honor the importance of grieving. That's because you need to mourn the end of the relationship that you and your ex once had in order to welcome the new, befriended relationship that you can build postdivorce.

The truth is that if you actively process loss and grief, you will find yourself reinvigorated for the life and love that are still to come. Human beings are especially resilient. An enduring wonder of human nature is that people respond to adversity in incredibly different ways. This chapter will help you understand the process of active, healthy grieving and guide you to experience your unique pathway to resiliency.

We Are Wired to Grieve Our Losses

Whether you like it or not, whether you left or were left, you are neurologically primed to experience loss after divorce. A more acute sense of loss is yours if you were the one who was left, but leaving, too, can result in a feeling of loss. Scientists who study love, such as anthropologist Helen Fisher (2004), have gathered data about how the brain responds to strong love emotions. When love is thwarted, Fisher discovered, a part of the brain that produces the chemical dopamine becomes activated. Brain scans of people who were recently rejected by their romantic partners suggest that excessive dopamine is produced during that time, making the person who was rejected become frantic and feel hopeless and depressed.

Grief Is Painful and Meaningful

Grieving forces us to face what we have lost. For many people who are divorcing, admitting the depth of their loss is unbearable. Avoiding the work of grieving is one way to deny your loss and the depth of your previous attachment to your ex. It's not easy to truly acknowledge that we've lost something we once wanted. Nor is it easy to admit having failed at something as important as marriage. Remember, though, wherever there is pain, there is also an opportunity for growth. And befriending your ex is a tremendous opportunity for growth.

Grief Is Essential to Resiliency

Active grieving requires the hard work of soul searching, which involves admitting to disappointment and failure, but it's an essential part of developing resiliency. Most of us don't know what healthy grieving looks and feels like, because we live in a culture that prioritizes coping and surviving. From childhood, many people have learned to turn away from their own pain, losses, and vulnerabilities. How often have you heard the following expressions?

- "If life gives you lemons, make lemonade."

- "Keep a stiff upper lip."

- "Just get on with it!"

- "Don't sweat the small stuff—and it's all small stuff!"

Listen to the resistant voices from clients in my office:

- "Me, mourn? I'm so happy to be done with her!"

- "After what he did to me? I feel like throwing a celebration party!"

- "Thank goodness I'm out of that marriage. I'm ready to finally live again!"

Despite the "get over it" messages you may receive from friends and family, know that psychologically, grief is a healthy and natural response. It's important to acknowledge that while you may be genuinely happy to be out of a marriage that didn't work, you simultaneously may be doing the work of mourning. At a myriad of unexpected moments, feelings of loss and grief may wash over you.

Many people avoid grieving by keeping busy. Ironically, crying is often seen as a sign of weakness, yet it's the body's way of expressing wordless pain. And the pain of divorce is often just that: wordless and overwhelming. Often I remind my clients of the story of Adam and Eve, who received the gift of weeping when they were expelled from the Garden of Eden. In other words, weeping is a gift to help us cope with sadness, loss, and the imperfect world in which we all live (Leick and Davidsen-Nielsen 1991).

Developing Resiliency

Resiliency has to do with your ability to bounce back from difficult experiences, adversity, challenges, or traumatic events, including family and relationship problems. Being resilient doesn't mean that you don't experience difficulty or distress; it means that you find creative solutions to problems, such as befriending your ex. On the contrary, the road to resilience will likely involve considerable emotional distress. Coping with emotional distress in healthy ways is the bedrock of what experts now refer to as *traumatic resilience* (Bonanno 2004).

Experts (ibid.) agree that a combination of personal traits contributes to resiliency. Having caring and supportive relationships within and outside the family plays a major role in resiliency. Other traits include having a positive view of yourself, confidence in your strengths and abilities, the capacity to make realistic plans and take the steps to carry them out, skills in communicating and problem solving, and the capacity to manage strong feelings. These traits, all of which you can learn and develop, are addressed throughout this book.

Resilience in the face of difficulties, including divorce, is more common than previously believed. Contrary to Judith Wallerstein and her colleagues' early research (Wallerstein and Blakeslee 1989, 2003; Wallerstein, Lewis, and Blakeslee 2000) on the damaging impact of divorce on children, data from Constance Ahrons (1994), Robert Emery (2004), and Mavis Hetherington and John Kelly (2002) found that resiliency in the face of divorce is the norm rather than the exception. Including a befriended ex as part of your support system is one pathway that can enhance your journey.

You Will Move through Loss in Your Own Way

It's important to remember that there's no one correct way to grieve anything, especially a divorce. For some people, divorce is an uncomfortable experience; for others, an extremely disturbing event; and for still others, a potential trauma. Some people suffer intensely for a short period of time and then settle down. Others experience acute distress from which they are unable to recover. Still others recover quickly but then begin to experience unexpected health problems, and find themselves having difficulty with concentrating on or enjoying life as they once did. Large numbers of people manage to cope with the temporary upheaval of divorce in a healthy way and seem able to manage new challenges with apparent ease. It's important to respect that you and your ex may approach the challenge of active grieving differently and therefore may be on different timetables for befriending. Be patient with yourself and your ex.

After 9/11, I ran a survivors group for widows. This was one of the most meaningful experiences of my professional life: witnessing the healing process of "healthy" traumatized people. One of the most powerful lessons I learned from running this group was that healthy grieving is achieved in different ways by different people. Several members of the group used journals to record their feelings while others never wrote a word. One woman moved back in with her mother after losing her husband, a solution that would have been damaging to another group member.

I was especially struck by the comparison between widows Veronica and Joan, who were both in their midthirties and had children aged nine and twelve. Veronica returned to work one week after 9/11, explaining, "I needed to return to work; it stabilized me." Joan stayed in bed for four months before returning to work. Yet six months after the towers fell, both women came to the group and reported having gone on their first dates since their husbands had died. People find different ways to nurture themselves in the face of loss. One size does not fit all. Although Veronica and Joan took entirely different pathways of mourning, both were equally *resilient.*

The Four Steps to Healthy Grieving

In the process of befriending your ex, you are faced with two tasks: simultaneously letting go of your old marital relationship and creating a new, befriended one. The tasks aren't discrete phases, but intertwine and overlap with one another. Often it may seem as if you have completed one phase until you discover that it needs to be repeated several times. Grief expert William Worden (2009) postulates that grief work may be divided into four steps that a mourner must complete. The four steps are:

1. Recognize, name, and accept the reality of the loss.

2. Release the emotions of grief.

3. Adjust to the new environment.

4. Invest emotional energy in new activities and relationships.

If the overall process sounds overwhelming, it is. The *work* of grieving becomes more accessible if we separately examine each of the four steps.

Step 1: Recognize, Name, and Accept the Reality of the Loss

Divorce allows for much practice in the "art of losing." Grieving involves mourning not only the marriage you have lost, but also the hopes, dreams, and expectations you once had for a life lived "happily ever after" with the person who is now your ex. Divorce insists on goodbyes. Active grieving begins with taking an inventory of your losses.

Exercise 3.1 Take a Loss Inventory

When conducting this exercise with my clients, I gently remind them that we all miss people who were once important to us, and I ask them to join me in this guided imagery:

> *Take a moment to think about how you felt when you met your ex: when you began dating, when you married, when your first child was born. What exactly was it about this person that appealed to you? What did your ex represent to you? What kind of life did you dream of building together? Life is always filled with pluses and minuses, gains and losses, dreams and delusions. Allow yourself to recall some of the ways that your ex once met your dreams, fantasies, desires, hopes.*

Jot down what came up for you during this process. Although it may be painful, in my experience, naming your losses is ultimately helpful. Being mindful of the things that drew you to your ex will help you accept and process the reality of the loss of your marriage, eventually making it easier for you to befriend your ex.

Here are some examples of losses my divorced clients have faced:

- Loss of companionship and shared experiences (which may or may not have been consistently pleasurable)

- Loss of financial support

- Loss of the social life that you shared as a couple

- Loss of the social acceptance that comes with being part of a couple

- Loss of hopes, plans, and dreams you had as a couple (which can be even more painful than practical losses)

- Loss of a partner to lean on

- Loss of a partner to fight with

- Loss of a known future

- Loss of your ex's extended family

- Loss of material possessions that have actual or sentimental value

- Loss of the opportunity to repair the relationship

Even though it may feel scary, take a moment to allow yourself to name and recognize the many losses that you are facing. The important thing is to give yourself permission to accept that these losses matter.

Many people fear that if they acknowledge and name their losses, their emotional response will be too intense to bear or they'll be stuck in a dark place forever. However, what I have learned is that the opposite is true. Being able to sit with your feelings of loss and grief is exactly what you need in order to move on to befriending your ex.

If any of the examples you've read about in this chapter have brought up any sadness that you've tried hard to avoid dealing with, now might be a good time to learn to sit with this feeling. You may want to develop a safe place inside yourself where you can go when your sad feelings are activated.

Exercise 3.2 Find a Safe Place

I use this exercise to teach my clients to develop a safe inner sanctuary where they can process grief.

> *Imagine yourself in a comfortable, peaceful, relaxing place.*
> *This place can be real or imaginary, somewhere you've been*
> *before, in reality or a fantasy; it may even be from a movie*
> *or a book. Let the image of the place emerge: a place that*
> *is peaceful, calm, and serene; a special inner place for you;*
> *someplace where you feel at ease, where you feel safe and*
> *secure; someplace that can be a sanctuary; somewhere to*
> *go to be quiet and reflective; somewhere special and healing*
> *for you. When you have found your safe place, explore and*
> *experience it: just notice the sounds, smells, and colors that*
> *you experience. Notice what it's like to be there. Allow yourself*
> *to absorb the feelings of peacefulness. Immerse yourself in*
> *this place of calmness and serenity. Now, let this place go,*
> *knowing that you can come back and access it whenever you*
> *want to.*

It's best to do this exercise when you feel calm. Reread the exercise to yourself and identify your safe place in your journal. This is a space that you can return to when you are dealing with difficult feelings.

A safe place doesn't necessarily have to be quiet and serene. One of my clients identified the tennis court! Other safe places that people have imagined include:

- A favorite coffeehouse

- The bed

- A movie theater

- A basement carpentry shop

- A friend's kitchen

My experience with divorced clients, my friends, and myself is that naming your losses facilitates acceptance of the new reality of your life. The pain of grief is precisely what helps you let go of the old relationship and move on to a befriended relationship. And no matter how strong your grief is, it won't last forever. Give yourself permission to recognize and feel loss, sadness, and grief.

Step 2: Release Grief

Grieving the death of a marriage is like mourning any loss: it hurts a lot, and you get through it minute by minute. Your job is to allow yourself to feel the pain. Your painful emotions may include anger, sadness, fear, panic, and loneliness. You may need to remind yourself that feelings aren't always logical and that's okay.

Talk. Talking is one important way to express your feelings. Friends, family, colleagues, and strangers can all be immensely helpful to you in releasing your grief. You may find a local face-to-face support group for divorced people or an online group. Talking even a few times to a therapist, counselor, coach, or clergyperson is another viable option. What's important is taking an active role by consciously pursuing a connection with another human being with whom you feel comfortable discussing your emotions.

Cry. Crying is another way to release feelings. The exercises in this book are designed to help you process your emotions. As you read and write, deep emotions may be evoked, which allows them to be released. Although you may have learned that crying is equivalent to "falling apart," I encourage you to allow yourself to cry when you feel like it. A scene from *The Prince of Tides* (Conroy and Johnston 1991) comes to mind. Tom Wingo is mourning his brother's death and has trouble crying. He asks, "Why cry? It won't bring him back." The therapist answers, "No, but it might bring you back."

Write. Another way to experience the pain of grief is by writing. Take a moment to be mindful of how you are feeling right now. You may want to jot down the feelings, thoughts, images, and sensations you are having as you allow yourself to feel your pain. It's important to be able to identify, feel, and simply sit with your emotions. Just notice whether you have any judgments about what comes up. If you find yourself being self-critical, see if you can let those thoughts go. Just notice what it's like to be with whatever you are feeling. If you have trouble accessing your feelings, try playing some music. Sometimes a piece of music can help you simply be with your feelings.

Move. In addition to releasing feelings verbally, our bodies offer other important avenues for releasing sorrow, grief, and anger. When we exercise, our bodies release endorphins, commonly known as the body's innate "feel-good" chemicals. Moving can shift your mood. Discover new ways to get your body moving or to practice being present in your body. Join a gym or a hiking club; sign up for yoga or kickboxing classes; or even put on music, pull down the shades, and dance around your house. Some people find that massage or acupuncture sessions are helpful for accessing the difficult emotions they may be unconsciously holding in their bodies.

Learn. Don't expect to finish mourning. You may never have complete closure, because your divorce will always affect you. The key is to learn from your losses and hurts in a way that enables you to respond by creating a healthy life. Finally, learn all you can about grief and, in particular, divorce-related grief. Reading can offer a unique kind of comfort and can help you feel less alone.

Step 3: Adjust to Your New Environment

You will need strength, perseverance, and hard work to make the transition from being married to being divorced. It's not something that will happen overnight, and it may take a few or several months, or even years, for the grief to hit. In all likelihood, you will experience a change in your lifestyle, schedule, responsibilities, and role in your family. Even if you are happy to be divorced, be prepared to face some empty moments. Know that it's common to feel an intense longing for the marriage you have lost, even if much of it was turbulent or distressing. Know that although isolation can feel unbearable, these feelings will eventually pass.

Develop a strong support system. It's tremendously important to develop a strong support system and draw on those people who can concretely help you as you adjust to your new life. For example, getting your kids off to school in the mornings, picking them up, and organizing their after-school schedules may place new burdens on you as you juggle some responsibilities that you once shared with your ex.

Exercise 3.3 Identify a Support Network

Think about the people in your life who have supported you so far and offered to help: family, friends, neighbors, and others who may have gone through or may be going through a divorce. Jot down their names in your journal. Now, make a second list of all the things you need help with; they may be practical activities, like mowing the lawn, or emotionally enriching responses, like listening to you on the phone, over a drink, or on a walk.

Scan these two lists and imagine yourself asking each person on the first list for help with the tasks on the second list. What do you notice as you do this exercise? Jot down your impressions. Can you imagine calling on these people? This is the time to surround yourself with as many caring people as possible. Make it your goal to ask one person a week for help with one of the things on your list.

Tap into your reservoir of positive experiences. Connecting with and reclaiming your positive experiences after losing your marital relationship is empowering. Everyone has had positive experiences that involved hobbies, places, people, or pastimes. Perhaps some of yours have been drummed out of you by the withering of your marriage. Now is the time to reach back to a positive memory of your life before you were married so that you can reclaim those positive experiences that are still part of you.

For example, it can be helpful to visit a place where you lived before you were married. Look around. Remind yourself of what you enjoyed doing when you lived in that particular place. Reaching out to connect with old friends whom you knew before your marriage and with whom you have lost touch is a way to reclaim past positive relationships. Even taking up an old hobby again can be strengthening. If it's not physically possible to reclaim these places, people, and activities, reimagining them is equally effective.

The following are some examples of how people have used positive memories to help them find strength after divorce:

Wen remembered the happy times she'd had visiting her grandmother in the Chinese countryside. When she remembered her grandmother's wonderful cooking, she began re-creating the recipes; their taste and smell brought back memories, and helped Wen reclaim herself as the confident, curious person she had been as a child.

Erich remembered how important soccer had once been in his life. After he was married, there never seemed to be enough time to play. He dusted off his old cleats and began to play several times a week in an amateur soccer league. This activity not only helped Erich reclaim his role of avid sportsman from his early twenties, but also gave him an outlet for physical exercise and helped him experience the camaraderie of a new group of friends.

Therese had lived a full and independent life in a different town from the one where she lived while married. One Saturday, she drove to her old town and parked in front of her old apartment building. She remembered how she had juggled three jobs and carried on an active social life when she lived there. She recalled the relaxed way that she and her roommate had related to one another and the rambunctious parties they'd organized. Then she walked up and down the main street. A few of the old shops were still there; the proprietor of the old hardware store was still there and remembered her! Therese felt renewed as she drove home from her old town.

Next, she got in touch with her old roommate; marriage and kids had allowed the two women to drift apart. They met for dinner, and as they caught up on each other's lives, Therese discovered that they could still talk for hours about everything and buoy one another's spirits. Therese laughed more freely than she had in a long time. When she and her old roommate hugged good-bye that evening and promised to stay in touch, Therese felt stronger and better supported for having revived an important friendship from her past.

Exercise 3.4 Reclaim Positive Experiences

Go back in time and recall activities that you used to find fun. See yourself having positive experiences before you were married, before you even knew your ex, and go back there.

All of us have within us a reservoir of positive experiences. Even if you are having a terrible time with a particular aspect of your divorce, you have undoubtedly had times in your life that were not fraught with trauma or pain. Being able to access these memories will help you heal.

Step 4: Invest Emotional Energy in New Activities and Relationships

As painful as active grieving can be, in the long run it frees up energy that you had been using in either the marriage or the divorce process. This energy is what you will need to invest in creating your new, post-divorce befriended relationship. Getting used to your new phone number, reorganizing the kitchen to familiarize yourself with the locations of pots and pans, and gaining confidence with driving in the snow are all small steps that are nonetheless significant markers in your new journey.

In a sense, your entire postdivorce life is about investing your energy in finding new meaning in your life. This is the time to do the things you may have always wanted to do: learn Italian, take up karate or watercolor painting, travel to a foreign country. It's an excellent time in your life to volunteer for an organization that needs your help, sign up for adult-education classes, or join a new club. Even small things can have a big impact: planting an herb garden, befriending a neighbor, trying out a new hairstyle. All these investments of emotional energy will expand your horizons and bring you new satisfaction. As a result of having moved on in your own life, you will have an easier time befriending your ex, and he will be more likely to consider you an appealing person to befriend.

As a general rule, it's better not to jump into a new serious relationship immediately after your divorce. While as Barbra Streisand reminded us in the song she made famous, "People," you do need other people, you first need time to process the loss and mourn the end of your marriage. You also need time to get to know the new "you."

A few years after her divorce, forty-two-year-old June told our divorce group how she avoided the task of mourning by "rushing around like crazy with anyone! Really, I tried to fill in the hole in my soul with anyone available!" The advice she gave others was "Don't rush!" This doesn't mean you should sit at home and brood, or feel lonely. You will know when you are ready to date. But recognize that the period after a divorce is not the time to make a permanent commitment to a new relationship.

Conclusion

Divorce always involves multiple losses: it's important to remember that grief is a normal response to loss and that active grieving will help you cope with your losses. Everyone grieves on her own timetable: for most people, sad feelings generally wane, but for some, a muted form of grief around losing a marriage continues throughout a lifetime. Acknowledging and actively grieving your losses, accessing your inner strengths, and building a strong support system are key to creating a resilient life.

In the next chapter, you'll learn more about another difficult emotion that hinders the befriending process: anger. Learning to be mindful about how you express your anger is also a hallmark of resiliency and a key to befriending your ex.

CHAPTER 4

when anger prevents befriending

On a chilly Monday morning in December, Hank read a surprising e-mail from Jenny, his ex.

Hi Hank,

> *I'm really sorry to tell you, but I won't be able to take the kids the week of Christmas break. My boss insists I work that week in our Las Vegas office, and although, truly, I'd rather be with the kids, I really can't say no to him. I could be fired, and besides, it's a great opportunity for me. Las Vegas is filled with new client possibilities that week. I know you will probably be pissed, but I wanted to give you a heads-up as soon as I got this news that I won't be able to keep the kids that week.*

> *—Jen*

"You will probably be pissed" was an understatement. As Hank reread the e-mail, he could feel his head pounding and his hands sweating. *Oh no, you bitch, you're doing it to me again!* This had been his year to have the kids for Christmas, but Jenny had begged him to switch Thanksgiving (her week) and Christmas (his week). He hadn't wanted to switch because Christmas was his favorite holiday, but as usual, he'd wanted to be a good guy. Since he wouldn't have the kids, he and his new girlfriend decided they would spend Christmas with her family in Texas, and now two weeks before Christmas Jenny was asking him—no, telling him—to switch back.

And then he noticed something else: she'd written the e-mail at 1:00 a.m. Instead of having the common decency to call him during regular hours and talk about this situation, she'd e-mailed! Who did she think she was, anyway? Within moments, he fired off an insulting e-mail to Jenny, which led her to reply with equally combative remarks. Another round of e-mails provoked him to call her, which led to one of their long, vicious phone calls replete with screaming.

Although you may never have been in this exact situation, is there anything about this emotionally explosive scenario that sounds familiar? Do you identify more with Hank or Jenny? Have you ever avoided a direct confrontation only to pay the price later? Have you ever fired off a nasty e-mail in a moment of anger? Jot down in your journal any memories that this situation brings up.

When we are under high levels of stress, our rational thinking and decision-making abilities go out the window. We say and do things impulsively and carelessly. Stress can easily overwhelm our minds and bodies, getting in the way of our ability to accurately read a situation, or stay aware of our own feelings and needs and communicate them effectively. And getting divorced undoubtedly will bring many new stressful situations into your life. Clearly, both Hank and Jenny were under stress. Neither behaved in ways that would further the thoughtful, collaborative postdivorce relationship they had finally, after two years, begun to build.

Difficult feelings are inevitable in any intimate relationship, and dealing with your ex is likely to bring up a whole range of strong, difficult feelings, anger being one of the most common. After all, the two of you were once married and know how to push each other's buttons! In this chapter I'll focus on how to deal with your anger. The strategies I recommend for dealing with anger are useful for many other difficult emotions. My goal is to help you understand how coping constructively with your anger and other difficult feelings can help you move forward in befriending your ex. Remember that what you learn about managing your anger is bound to apply to your future relationships as well.

Few people get divorced without feeling angry. In fact, divorce is a hotbed of anger, resentment, bitterness, and other uncomfortable feelings. If you are like most people who divorce, learning to deal with these difficult feelings toward your ex is a big part of the work you will have to do to create a collaborative relationship. Unhealed wounds that may have collected over years may easily fuel conflict in your current situation. And the anger you or your ex vent, whether justifiable or not, can easily become a source of new wounding and a rehearsal for future angry conflict.

Anger Is a Natural Reaction

According to anger expert Harriet Lerner (1985), anger is natural, and a certain amount of anger is necessary for survival. Yet too many of us try to bury our anger or discharge it in impulsive outbursts.

Psychologist Daniel Goleman (1995) defines what he calls a "family of anger" that involves a spectrum of feelings including irritation, annoyance, outrage, resentment, frustration, wrath, fury, rage, hostility, and hatred. These are feelings that many people think of as negative and thus want to avoid experiencing. Other people feel themselves drowning in a bottomless pool of anger that never abates. The bottom line is that anger is a signal worth listening to and allowing yourself to feel. The key is what you *do* with your anger. Difficult emotions can be a source of either growth or pain. Although it's not easy, learning to use your emotions in constructive ways can help you grow and change, and befriend your ex.

A Balanced Approach to Handling Anger

Generally, there are two schools of thought when it comes to the healthiest way to handle your anger.

The "let it all hang out" school of thought—epitomized by Arthur Janov (1970), creator of *primal scream therapy*, which was popularized three decades ago—advocates the importance of unearthing and releasing anger. This perspective emphasizes how harboring angry feelings without expressing them can lead to a host of psychological and physical problems, such as depression and high blood pressure, and inhibits feeling joy.

The opposing viewpoint emphasizes containing your anger (Paleg and McKay 2001). This school of thought believes that anger feeds on itself, that expressing anger only makes you angrier, raises your blood pressure, activates your nervous system, increases your stress level, and likely damages you or others.

Each of these two viewpoints has some value and some cost. Repressing anger can make us sick, but so can expressing it. Every situation you face demands reflection.

You actually know your ex quite well, and it's up to you to use this knowledge to plan your strategy. Is your ex the kind of person who will ignore you when you make a gentle request, only responding to angry outbursts or vicious threats? Or is he the kind of person for whom a vicious threat will get you nowhere? No one viewpoint is correct all the time, and the solution is sometimes expressing and other times containing your anger. Finding what works in each unique situation is an important challenge.

But one thing is fairly certain: befriending your ex is likely to evoke some angry feelings. Impulsive eruptions are damaging, but so is holding in too much. Although problems with anger may involve or even be triggered by your ex, since you have no control over the other person, the only thing you can do is work on yourself.

Learning healthy ways to express anger will help you reach your postdivorce vision of a friendly relationship with your ex. In addition, learning healthy ways to express anger can help you feel better physically and emotionally, and bring more authenticity and intimacy into your life. What's important to remember is that the key to handling anger effectively is to find a balance between expressing your feelings and keeping them to yourself.

Here's an analogy that works for many of my clients: When I taught my children to drive, I learned a lot about them and myself as well. When, my first child, my son, was behind the wheel, I found myself cringing and clinging to the passenger door as I felt the car speeding out of control. I told him, "The brakes! Step on the brakes!" Four years later, when my daughter learned to drive, I had the opposite experience: I found myself reminding her, "The gas! Give it the gas!"

Just as you learn how to drive a car by stepping carefully on the gas pedal to pick up speed and then stepping carefully on the brake pedal when it's necessary to slow down or stop, you can learn how to balance your emotional reactions by stepping on the gas (expressing yourself) or the brakes (keeping your feelings to yourself) at appropriate times.

Evaluating Your Anger

To find this balance between stepping on the gas pedal and braking, you must first assess and learn more about your own style of anger. The following two exercises will help you do that.

Exercise 4.1 How Do You Handle Being Angry at Your Ex?

Think about the last time you got angry at your ex. Ask yourself: *What happened to me when I got so angry? How do I feel about my own behavior? What other emotions was I feeling at the time? Did I feel hurt, guilty, wronged, or wrong? How did I handle my feelings? Did I need to step on the brakes, or gas it?*

Jot down what came up for you when you considered these questions. Now, imagine handling the situation without anger. Write down what you would do differently and how it might affect your relationship with your ex. Remember, it's up to you to manage your anger. You have a choice: step on the gas pedal or pump the brakes.

Exercise 4.2 Your Anger Management Style

This exercise will help you understand more about your style of handling anger. Circle the number of each statement that applies to you:

1. I rarely tell someone I'm angry at her. If I did, I'd feel too vulnerable.

2. I worry that if I let my anger out, I'll pay for it.

3. I often cut people out of my life when they make me angry.

4. When I get angry, I yell, throw things, and say horrible things that I later regret.

5. I recently got so angry that I punched a hole in the wall.

6. People tell me that I "leak" anger as opposed to being open about my feelings.

7. I usually express my anger after I sit on it for a while and calm down.

8. When I'm angry, I write in my journal to get a hold on my feelings.

9. When I'm angry, I feel better if I go to the gym or take a run.

10. I try to avoid blaming others when I'm angry.

11. If someone is angry at me, I try to listen to the person's feelings without retaliating.

12. I find it helpful to speak with a good friend when I'm really angry.

If you circled the first six statements, you may need some help learning to manage your anger. Circling statements 1, 2, and 3 suggests that you need some help with stepping gently on the gas pedal to express your anger. Circling statements 4, 5, and 6 suggests that you need help with stepping firmly on the brakes and containing your anger.

If you marked the last six statements, you are probably able to cope with your angry feelings in a healthy way.

Exercise 4.3 Handle Your Anger: The Past

Now review the anger inventory in the previous exercise and reread the last six statements. Imagine what might have transpired if you had used any of those last six approaches when you became angry at your ex. What might the outcome have been? Write about any of the positive behavioral tools described in that exercise that you would like to develop or reinforce.

Exercise 4.4 Handle Your Anger: The Future

Think about a possible upcoming situation with your ex of the type that usually makes you angry. For example, imagine if he brought the children back late or introduced them to a new love interest. Or imagine that he didn't return your phone call for a week. Choose an event, write it down, and, again, consider the last six statements in exercise 4.2. Based on what you learned previously about healthy tools for managing your anger, if this situation happens, what can you do to express your feelings without lashing out or making the situation worse? Jot down your responses in your journal.

Reacting vs. Responding

Hank and Jenny, whom we met at the beginning of this chapter, both provide good examples of what happens when people *react* rather than *respond*. You may use these two words synonymously, but they have different meanings.

- Reacting is acting impulsively from your gut feelings, by displaying intense emotions without self-censorship.

- Responding is noticing what you are feeling in your gut and then choosing an action that is healthy and balanced.

Keep in mind that responding doesn't have to involve words. For example, choosing *not* to engage in an argument when you are provoked can be a response.

Learning to respond rather than react is an important skill for all of us, especially if we are trying to build a good working relationship with an ex-spouse. It's a skill that enhances all our relationships for the rest of our lives, too, because:

- Speaking from a centered place calms us down.

- Describing and naming our feelings gives us a sense of power.

- When we respond (rather than react), we are more likely to act appropriately and be taken seriously.

Reacting

Many of us are habituated to reacting rather than responding. Although reacting can sometimes feel good (because there is a sense of release in discharging emotions), in general reacting doesn't help you build a befriended relationship. Responding involves taking the time to reflect, and reflecting on our lives often yields important insights. Let's look at the two main explanations that experts have found in their attempts to understand why people get stuck in reacting rather than responding.

Old scripts get replayed. Sigmund Freud (1922) was the first to identify the repetition compulsion, the pattern whereby people endlessly repeat distressing moments from early life. Freud believed that this repeating was an attempt to master the initial distressing event. Each time an event is reenacted, it is done with the hope of achieving a more satisfactory ending. This is often called "replaying old scripts," where people act out, rather than reflect on their experiences and choose more appropriate actions. Had Jenny and Hank (the couple whose story you read at the opening of this chapter) taken some time to reflect before responding to one another, they might have remembered how easily they were prone to fall into a nasty cycle. Had they remembered, they might have mourned the past, rather than replayed their old script and hurt one another again.

We are driven by our emotions. Another way to understand what happened to Hank and Jenny is what current neuropsychologists call an *amygdala hijack*. Coined by Daniel Goleman (1995) in his influential book *Emotional Intelligence: Why It Can Matter More Than IQ*, an "amygdala hijack" is when a person's emotional response suddenly takes over and she is unable to think rationally. The amygdala is the part of the brain that regulates emotions and memory. An amygdala hijack exhibits three signs: a strong emotional reaction, sudden onset, and the later realization that the reaction was inappropriate.

An amygdala hijack can happen in a millisecond. And what you choose in this millisecond is the key to controlling your reaction when anger-provoking events compel you to "lose it." *Lag time*, a concept first identified by neurosurgeon Benjamin Libet (2004), a pioneer in the field of human consciousness, refers to the time between when we get the urge to take action and when we actually take it. What this means is that by recognizing the *window of opportunity*, you have the power to disengage from a reactive urge.

Responding

How would the situation look if Jenny and Hank had been able to respond rather than react? If they could have followed the next two steps, this is what their situation would have looked like:

1. Describe what you are feeling.

Jenny: "I'm feeling pulled between my obligations to my job and my family."

Hank: "I'm feeling as if I constantly give in to you, and this time I refuse!"

2. Speak from a calm, centered place.

Jenny: "I wanted to give you advance notice. I just learned about this, and I'm scared that you'll be angry at me and blow up, as you have before. That's why I'm bringing it up—so that we can talk civilly."

Hank: "I would appreciate your calling me back or talking to me in person after you've slowed down."

If Jenny and Hank had been aware of the window of opportunity, they might have taken the time to pause and reflect before contacting one another.

The significance of the window of opportunity is extraordinary. Being aware of this lag time allows you to take a deep breath and savor the opportunity that exists in the moment when you choose your response to something your ex says or does that makes you feel angry. A split second is enough time to remember that to get along with your ex, you need to think before reacting, and learn to respond rather than react. I will emphasize this concept repeatedly throughout this book. Using the mindful-breathing techniques introduced in chapter 2 will help you slow down and respond, rather than react, to your anger.

Exercise 4.5 How to Respond Rather Than React

Think about whether you usually resort to reacting rather than responding when you are interacting with your ex. Most of us who have been divorced have moments that we aren't proud of and that, if we had the chance, we would handle with more wisdom and maturity.

This two-step writing exercise will help you see how your anger triggers your emotional reactions and prompts your specific behaviors.

1. **Make three columns in your journal.** Label the columns "Event," "Emotion," and "Behavior." List a few situations or events that have made you angry with your ex, the specific emotion you experienced (irritation, annoyance, rage), and

how you behaved (verbal outburst, self-restraint, sarcasm). Remember two important things:

- Emotions are not unhealthy; it's the unhealthy behaviors that we want to change.

- None of us is perfect, and in fact, divorce brings out the worst in most people.

2. **Visualize changing one behavior.** From the list you just made, choose one *behavior* of yours that you wish had never occurred. Recall the event that triggered the behavior, keeping in mind that although we are powerless to control events, we can change our reactions to them. As you think back, consider whether using mindful breathing might have been helpful. How might it have helped you re-center yourself and delay your reaction? We can't change the past or predict the future, but we can practice calming down.

Right now, use mindful breathing as you recall this event. Notice whether just using mindful breathing helps you calm down, and whether calming down helps you think of alternative behaviors you might have used. For this exercise, it's enough to imagine how deep breathing might have changed your behavior. Here's how some of my clients responded:

- Fran proudly said, "I was able to imagine gently and firmly telling my ex, 'I'm losing it right now; I need to stop talking about this. I'll call you back in the morning.'"

- Bill reported that after practicing deep breathing, he was able to visualize telling his ex, "I can't make a decision in the heat of the moment. Let me think over your suggestion and get back to you in a few days."

- Rhebai said, "Deep breathing made me see how unimportant the whole argument was, and in my imagination, I was able to walk away."

Feelings Are Fine: It's Reacting That Gets You into Trouble

Let's take yet another look at what went wrong between Hank and Jenny. Perhaps Jenny shot off an e-mail as quickly as possible to avoid feeling guilty about asking for a last-minute schedule change. Perhaps after years of explosions with Hank, some of which were her doing and some his, she'd decided to try to avoid a confrontation. Perhaps she was scared of creating a new conflict. Perhaps all of these concerns were operating. Sometimes, even in retrospect and on reflection, it's hard to sort out the multiple threads affecting our decisions.

It's possible that Hank experienced a combination of anger and many of its layers and nuances: rage, bitterness, resentment, and annoyance. Perhaps he was feeling that once again, he was being asked to cater to Jenny. He may have also felt frustration and anxiety about communicating within his new relationship; wouldn't his new girlfriend be disappointed, even resentful?

Again, it wasn't their feelings that got Hank and Jenny in trouble but their reactions. Both of them needed to take some time to pause, breathe, and respond, rather than react. Both needed to be committed to understanding their feelings and get to the bottom of them before communicating. Both needed to keep their befriended relationship a priority and take the high road. You will meet Jenny and Hank in the next chapter again and see if they learned anything from reacting, rather than responding.

Conclusion

Divorce is often a hotbed of anger. Your biggest challenges are to:

1. Notice, identify, and honor your angry feelings.

2. Avoid reacting impulsively and instead choose to respond mindfully.

In this chapter I have stressed that it's not your feelings that get you into trouble, but what you do with them. While angry emotions don't feel good, it's important to allow yourself to feel your feelings and to find healthy ways of expressing the needs behind your anger, especially when your anger interferes with befriending.

An important concept to remember is the amygdala hijack; be aware of how reacting, rather than responding, to the amygdala hijack can get you in trouble, and remember the power of the split-second window of opportunity. Keep in mind two points about expressing anger:

- Anger begets anger.

- Continuous explosions of anger at your ex can keep you tied to the unsatisfying relationship that you had before your divorce.

In the next chapter we will look more carefully at the process of letting go of your angry feelings, as well as other aspects of letting go. Part of forming a friendly relationship with your ex means learning to let go of old roles, expectations, and feelings while creating a new relationship.

CHAPTER 5

letting go

Ernesto and Tanya moved in together the summer after their high-school graduation, when she became pregnant. He found a job at a copy shop, where he could work the night shift and take care of their baby girl, Carla, while Tanya worked during the day. He tried to ignore Tanya's constant criticisms: he didn't dress the baby appropriately, forgot Tanya's birthday, and never did the dishes. She complained bitterly that they never had fun anymore. Ernesto felt as if he could do nothing right.

When Carla was eighteen months old, Tanya decided she'd had enough. She told Ernesto she was moving out. She was moving in with her mother, who would watch Carla during the day while she was working and at night so that Tanya could go out. She needed more personal space. She was too young to commit to one person.

Ernesto was shaken to the core. They'd never married, and legally he had no rights, even though he dearly loved Carla. But true to his personal style, he took this news passively and silently, as he had taken most of Tanya's decisions and opinions. He clenched and unclenched his fists, and set his jaw in stoic acceptance. Inside, however, he felt anxiety building. He broke out in a sweat and then got the chills.

What was he going to do now? Tanya had been his best friend; more than that, he depended on her for everything from deciding what groceries to buy to paying the bills, and generally as his guide, especially when it came to raising Carla. When Tanya walked out, he second-guessed his every decision: How would Tanya handle this? What would she think if he did that? Sometimes he felt panicked and crazed: how would he survive without her?

After Tanya moved out, he continued to text her, sometimes sending twenty messages a day. If he didn't hear back from her immediately, he felt anxious, and his imagination began running wild. He pictured the baby as injured, and Tanya at the emergency room. Or maybe the house had burned down. Maybe she had fallen for another guy—and he would never see Tanya or Carla again! They might move to another state—or country! The longer it took for her to respond, the more anxious he became. His signature text message (which Tanya ignored) was "Are U ok? Write 2 me!!!!!"

One day he got a message from Tanya: "U R too much! Get over it. We R not together. Leave me alone. Let go!!" When he read that text message, Ernesto went into the bathroom and threw up.

Whether you identify with Ernesto or Tanya, you can see that both are hurting. Even though they are behaving in opposite manners (Ernesto feels abandoned and acts clingy, and Tanya feels suffocated and acts dismissive), neither has separated from the other in a way that promotes befriending.

To befriend your ex, you must come to terms with the fact that your marital relationship has ended. You need to be committed to letting go and "wiping the slate clean." Even if you feel disappointed, dismayed, depressed, and defeated, you need to wipe the slate clean. This doesn't mean forgetting the past you've shared with your ex; it means consciously deciding to begin again. You consciously decide to put the past where it belongs and start anew with a clean slate.

Like most things worth doing, this is easier said than done. To befriend your ex, you both must learn a new way to interact and communicate. As I mentioned in the previous chapter, since you have no control over your ex the same principle applies: the only thing you can do is work on yourself.

On a deeper level, letting go means accepting that life is continually changing and all of our relationships are continually evolving. Growing into your new, befriended relationship may trigger stress and anxiety, but it can also nourish your strength.

Relationships Are Always Evolving

Once you decide to befriend your ex, you need to access the emotional "muscles" you've used in other relationships when you've let go of an old stage and ushered in a new one. These are the same muscles that will help you let go of your old relationship with your ex and form a befriended relationship. The parent-child relationship is a good example of a relationship that sustains many evolutions and transitions. So consider how your relationship with your parents has changed over time.

Across cultures, parents care for their children intensively during the early years of life. At some point, children naturally let go of their dependent roles and become more independent, just as parents naturally loosen their protective roles and trust their children to become autonomous. Midway through the life cycle, the caretaking relationship may become reversed. After children have grown up and parents start to age, many adult children assume caretaking responsibilities for their now-dependent parents. These transitions, which are normal and expected, involve letting go of old roles to evolve into new roles.

Friendship is another area of evolving relationships. Most of us have varied and changing friendships. We accept that our best buddies in elementary or high school may not necessarily be our closest adult friends. We may still enjoy meeting with an old friend who is no longer a close friend. A boss-employee relationship is another example of a relationship that may evolve into a personal friendship. We may develop close ties with a next-door neighbor, but when that neighbor moves across the country, both parties know that the friendship is in transition. Again, these transitions are normal and expected, and you rely on your capacity to let go of one role before expecting yourself to be able to move on to the next one.

Take a moment to reflect on how your relationships with your parents and various others—neighbors, high-school friends, and friends or bosses from work—may have evolved and what roles you have let go of. You may recognize various turning points; if so, note them in your journal.

Unfortunately, we have few healthy models that teach us how to transition out of one of the most important relationships of our lives: a troubled marriage. On the contrary, most of the stories we hear are about how divorced people are bitter enemies who spend a lifetime seeking vengeance or wallowing in sorrow. How ironic, because transitioning into a friendly relationship with a former spouse can offer you a great deal of satisfaction! But letting go of your old roles of husband and wife is a prerequisite to moving into a new, befriended relationship with one another. You may have already begun the journey of befriending; if so, note in your journal the old roles you have let go of.

Sometimes, old habits and attachments persist even when they are no longer useful. Signing the divorce papers and living separately doesn't always mean you have truly let go of your past relationship. Holding on to feelings of anger, guilt, or fear can make the transition more problematic. Although you may say that you are glad to be done with your ex-spouse, your actions may reveal that in reality, you are still holding on in a way that hinders your healing.

Exercise 5.1 Are You Having Trouble Letting Go?

To discover whether you're having trouble letting go of your marriage or your ex-spouse, do this self-assessment. In your journal, start a new section titled "Am I having trouble letting go of my ex?" Read the following list and rate each item "always," "sometimes," or "never." Copy into your journal any of the activities you rate as "always" or "sometimes."

1. Crying or drinking more than usual when you see or think about your ex

2. Talking a lot with friends and family about your ex's positive or negative qualities

3. Reacting with strong emotions (anger, sadness, or anxiety) to every interaction with your ex

4. Calling your ex about everyday issues, only to discover that he really isn't available or interested

5. Spending time thinking about old wounds involving your ex

6. Driving by your ex's house to check up on her

7. Asking your children for information about your ex's life

8. Yearning for sex with your ex

If you copied more than three items from the list, you may be having trouble letting go. If so, read on to gain some clarity. If you copied fewer than three items, you're doing a good job of letting go, but you can still gain clarity by reading on.

Letting Go of Past Expectations and Roles

In her essay "A Twenty-First Century Ritual," author Erica Jong (2006) wrote that when she became divorced, the three little words that scared her the most were not "I love you," but having to fill in "next of kin" on formal documents. Jong's confession acknowledges the existential pain of feeling alone in the world and the practicalities that accompany being without a significant other.

Yet divorce doesn't have to be an existential or practical disaster. If you and your ex are befriended, you may still offer and receive support from one another in many ways. It's equally important that you find additional mutual support systems. Sometimes it's tricky to find a healthy balance, but it can be done. My friend Bonnie visited her ex in the hospital when he had open-heart surgery. But she was not the one who took him there, spoke with the doctors, or supervised his postoperative treatments. It's a question of creating new boundaries and expectations.

Boundaries and Expectations

The boundaries and expectations that defined your life as a married person are no longer viable when you are divorced. For example, when you were married, you may have had the right to call or text your ex repeatedly and expect an answer, which is no longer the case after you are divorced. Now it's up to you to establish a new boundary and make do when your ex doesn't return your call. When you were married, you probably expected that if your car broke down, your spouse would come and get you. Now this is no longer a reasonable expectation. The ball is in your court to set up a new support system.

The following are two examples of how divorced people replaced their exes' support with support from other loved ones: Jack asked his brother, an English teacher, to proofread his résumé and job-query letters, a task that Jack's wife had previously done. Didi found another single mother on her street with whom to share carpooling. The two women agreed that they could call on one another if either expected to be late and the other woman's child needed a ride home from an after-school activity.

The task of defining a new support system, one that includes but is not limited to your ex, is now up to you.

The roles and expectations that you and your ex hold may change over time. As your children grow up, you will need a new blueprint for your relationship. For example, when your children are small and they suffer colds and the flu, you might expect your ex to go to the pharmacy to pick up medicine, because you don't want to leave a sick toddler alone in the house. By the time your child is a teenager, you won't need or expect that kind of help from your ex-spouse.

Roles

On the most obvious level, befriending is complicated. You are creating a new connection with a person with whom you have just gone through a process of disconnection and toward whom you may still feel hurt or angry. On a deeper level, befriending means letting go of your old relationship roles with the person you married while creating a new relationship with this very familiar person. It means coming to terms with the fact that "forever" was a myth. It means acknowledging that the person you married, the person you knew so well, has now moved out of your zone of influence. It means acknowledging that this person, your ex, is no longer your partner, and facing the fact that you are no longer bonded in the same way.

Letting go of old roles is a big challenge. To transform a relationship of intimacy (especially painful intimacy) to one of friendship and collaboration requires developing the capacity to let go of what isn't helping you and to hold on to what sustains you.

Here's a story from my own life about letting go of old roles and creating new ones. During our divorce, my soon-to-be ex and I spent a great deal of time, money, and anguish on our lawyers and weren't able to come to a financial settlement. My lawyer wanted to take the case to trial. Knowing the probable financial and familial repercussions of a trial and feeling desperate, I decided to risk trusting my own intuition. I called my ex and said, "Let's settle. We can figure this out ourselves."

My ex could have said, "No. I want to fight it out in court." In that case I would have reassured myself that at least I'd tried to do things differently. But to my good fortune, he, too, took a risk to avoid waging a court battle that was certain to fuel an adversarial relationship. From a willingness on both our parts to try out new roles came a moment of transformation, one that evolved into a growing befriended relationship. In our old roles we were adversaries who communicated through our lawyers. In our new roles we became two reasonable people whose marriage had dissolved. We sat down together and negotiated a compromise that we could both live with.

Soon after that, I received a huge bill from my lawyer. When I examined it, I noticed the enormous number of telephone charges she'd attributed to conversations with my ex's lawyer. Since we were now on better terms, I called my ex with my dilemma. We sat down, compared our two itemized bills, and discovered that I'd been billed for phone calls that were not on his lawyer's bill! With my ex's encouragement and coaching, I took another risk by confronting my lawyer and insisting that she reduce my bill. Another transformation occurred as I realized that my ex could be a supportive ally.

Letting go of past expectations and roles requires leaving behind the familiar and risking the unknown. Often people get stuck in a negative story. I could have easily gotten stuck in a victim role ("My lawyer is making me take him to court!"). Instead, I took a risk and let go of anticipating that my ex would be adversarial. Because I took a risk and thought outside the box, our relationship took a monumental leap for the better.

Take a moment to ask yourself:

- Is there an aspect of your relationship that isn't working well with your ex?

- Is there a risk you can take (even a small one) that might improve your relationship?

I routinely ask my clients those questions. Here are a couple of responses:

Herado was frantic when her son had a fever and her car was in the shop. Her ex, Jimmy, responded generously when she asked him to loan her his brand-new car to take their son to the doctor. Months later Jimmy borrowed Herado's futon when his sister came to town unexpectedly. Now the two have grown into the habit of loaning each other not only cars during emergencies but also a variety of household items.

In chapter 4 you met Jenny, who created a huge glitch when she e-mailed Hank late at night instead of sensitively discussing in person a request she knew he wouldn't like. Even though Jenny was uncomfortable asking directly for what she needed, the next time she was asked by her boss to work on a weekend when she was supposed to have the kids, she took a risk by calling Hank well in advance and politely explaining her situation. Hank was unavailable to take the kids that weekend, but he and Jenny put their heads together to figure out a solution. When Hank suggested that the kids stay with his sister, Beth, Jenny was overjoyed, and a new tradition began: the kids began sleeping at Aunt Beth's when neither Mom nor Dad was available.

You need to be mindful as you think through these types of decisions, and be emotionally prepared to endure the inevitable uncertainty in creating a new, befriended relationship with your ex.

In your postdivorce relationship with your ex, you will encounter many situations where the two of you will have the option to stretch by taking the risk of asking for or accepting support from one another. Much depends on the extent to which you are able to let go of your old roles and expectations, and redefine your relationship. As you read the next vignettes, think about how the different outcomes in these two similar situations might have been related to the exes' readiness to let go of old roles, attitudes, and expectations.

Melanie's daughter woke up with a fever and a cold the day Melanie had to deliver a big presentation at work. Melanie called her ex and told him her predicament. "I'll be right over," replied her ex, a graphic designer who worked from home. Melanie sighed with grateful relief. Her presentation went wonderfully that day, and soon afterward, her longed-for promotion came through.

Across town, Wendy's three-year-old woke with a fever, but Wendy had to be at work that day. Frantic, she called the day-care provider and related her predicament, but was reminded of the rules that disallowed any child with a fever from attending day-care. Even though they weren't on good terms, Wendy then called her ex. She knew it was his day off, and asked if he could possibly come over to take care of their sick child. "I already made plans for today," replied her disgruntled ex. Wendy hung up and burst into tears. She was upset not only that her ex wasn't available, but also that he seemed annoyed at hearing from her and didn't even apologize for being unable to help. She didn't feel right leaving her daughter with a babysitter under those conditions, and besides, who could come at such short notice? She called her boss and told him she wouldn't be able to come in that day.

Why do you think Melanie's ex was willing to help her out and Wendy's ex wasn't? The key word in the second vignette is "disgruntled." Clearly, Wendy's ex was holding on to some unpleasant feelings and attitudes about their relationship. The point here is that when a person feels disgruntled, angry, or resentful, it's likely that he won't be particularly friendly or helpful.

Exercise 5.2 Are You Ready to Let Go of Old Roles and Expectations?

Let's review your responses from the previous exercise. Look at the items you copied into your journal. For each item, answer these questions:

1. Has this behavior affected your relationship with your ex?

2. If you think about letting go of this behavior, what emotions do you experience? List them.

3. Are you ready to let go of this behavior? If not, why not?

4. If you answered yes to the previous question, list the steps you might take to move on from this behavior.

5. Think about how your life would look if you didn't engage in this behavior. Write down, in detail, how your life would be different.

If you answered no to question 3, then you need to spend more time working on releasing this issue.

The following are two techniques for you to practice that may serve as useful support, even if you feel unable to let go of your past relationship with your ex.

Techniques for Letting Go

Perhaps you are holding on to anger from past events. Remember that letting go is not the same as forgiving or forgetting. You don't have to forgive your ex for things that you feel are unforgivable: an extramarital affair, lying, verbal or physical abuse—the list goes on and on. However, what you do have to do is let go of ruminating about these events. Ruminating is an internal experience that has no effect on the other person and just makes you miserable. Learning how to step back from the emotions that are controlling you will help you let go. Your new befriended relationship is not about keeping past grievances and injustices alive, but about a shared relationship that you will have with your ex for years to come.

Learning to let go takes practice. The following two exercises can help you. Practicing either or both of them regularly can help you strengthen your "letting go muscles." These exercises can be especially helpful if you feel like engaging in some of the unhelpful activities that you copied from exercise 5.1 earlier in this chapter, or when something your ex does or says makes you feel upset.

Exercise 5.3 Leaves on the Water

Find a comfortable position, close your eyes, and take a few slow, deep breaths.

> *Imagine that you're sitting by the side of a gently flowing stream and there are leaves floating on the surface of the water. For the next five minutes, think of some of the behaviors you listed in exercise 5.1. Think of a recent or not-so-recent troubling interaction you had with your ex. Think of ways that you feel hurt by your ex or ways in which you miss your ex. Think of the kinds of things you ruminate about. As each thought, feeling, memory, or image comes into your mind, imagine placing it on a leaf and letting it float downstream.*

Before moving on to the next exercise, record your thoughts and feelings in your journal.

Exercise 5.4 All Crumpled Up

Think of something your ex has done that has made you feel angry, anxious, upset, or ashamed.

1. On a clean sheet of paper, write fast and furiously for five to ten minutes about the incident. Write it however you feel, using a red marker or capital letters for anger and tiny letters for shame, and don't hesitate to use plenty of exclamation marks and foul language. Don't hold back, and write as if

you were telling a story about the incident to a close and sympathetic friend.

2. When you have finished writing all you can about the event, take the piece of paper and crumple it into a small ball. If you feel more comfortable writing on a computer, print out the document and crumple that into a ball.

3. Put the crumpled piece of paper in an ashtray or a deep dish. Tear the paper into tiny pieces. Now, find a match and set it on fire. Watch the paper burn. Be sure to do this in a safe environment where you are not in danger.

Write about how you feel as you watch the paper turn into ashes and smoke.

Each of these exercises is designed to help you let go of whatever it is about your ex that keeps you holding on to your past relationship. The first exercise uses imagery; numerous studies (see, for example, Naparstek 1994) have demonstrated that imagining making a change helps us follow through with it. For example, athletes who imagine themselves making that winning basketball or tennis shot improve their games. The second exercise is based on the premise that the burning is both a concrete and a symbolic act of extinguishing and letting go of distressing emotions.

Keeping What Works

So far I have focused on helping you let go of unrealistic expectations and roles that keep you tied to your ex in unhealthy ways. Now, I want to switch gears and remind you that there may be many positive aspects of your married life that worked well. I'd like to help you explore what positive aspects of your marriage might be worth focusing on and actively integrating into your new, befriended relationship. This concept is summarized in the old saying, "Don't throw out the baby with the bathwater."

If there are simple routines or rituals from your marriage that can be carried over into your postdivorce relationship, then by all means try to preserve them. It can only help you and your relationship with your ex. This concept is best illustrated in the following touching story.

> When Janet and Rafael were married, one of their favorite Saturday morning rituals was sitting on the back stoop drinking coffee and watching their kids play on the jungle gym. One morning, Rafael came to pick up the kids at Janet's house (she'd stayed in the family home). She had just made a pot of coffee, and spontaneously offered Rafael a cup. He accepted, and was touched that she remembered that he liked extra sweetener. The two felt awkward at first, but gradually, as this discomfort diminished, they found themselves in their old spot on the back stoop and enjoying the kids, who, not coincidentally, were having fun showing off their latest stunts. This is a good example of taking one small step (as suggested in chapter 1) toward developing a befriended relationship with your ex.

> Sometimes, sustaining relationships with your ex's family can strengthen your attempts to befriend your ex. Charlene had always been close to her mother-in-law, Bess. They shared many common interests, spoke on the phone every week, and always seemed to find something to laugh about together. When Charlene and Jeremy divorced, Bess made Charlene promise that *their* relationship would remain intact. For the first few years after the divorce, Charlene and Bess carried on as before and, in fact, deepened their relationship. Charlene sought Bess's advice on problems she was having with the children, and occasionally Bess shared news about Jeremy. The fact that his mother and ex-wife were friends made Jeremy feel fairly comfortable about befriending Charlene as well. Bess always saw the best in people and encouraged others to do the same.
>
> Then Jeremy remarried, which worried Charlene. Now Bess had a new daughter-in-law to fuss over. Surely it would become awkward. But Charlene need not have worried. Her ex-mother-in-law called and cheerfully announced, "I want you to know that I now have one son and two daughters-in-law." Charlene and Bess's continuing relationship supported the continuance

of Charlene and Jeremy's befriended relationship even after Jeremy had remarried.

Many divorced people are surprised to find that when their exes are in trouble, they feel compelled to help. For example, when Claudia's father had a stroke, her ex not only watched the children so that she could spend time at the hospital, but also offered to drive Claudia back and forth, since he realized how distraught and anxious she was. Fred's ex came over to help him with the children when his new wife broke her leg.

These examples are not meant to illustrate "shoulds," but to illustrate how reasonable it is to expect an ex to extend herself for your children.

Accepting Your New Relationship with Your Ex

You may be wary of having to accept the person whose flaws and limitations you know only too well and found all too irritating. Although it might sound counterintuitive, it can actually be easier to accept your ex now that you are no longer married. Letting go of what went wrong and concentrating on the future allows you and your ex to focus on a limited and important relationship: co-parenting your children.

Letting Go of Past Accounting

It's hard to befriend someone when you dwell on his past mistakes and shortcomings. If you are having trouble letting go, perhaps you can relate to Jill, who recently came to my office. Divorced for eight years, she insisted on telling me what a loser her ex had been from day one. As evidence she cited his faulty financial decisions and how he couldn't hold a job and spent too much time drinking beer after work with his buddies. As she recounted their sad story, she even regaled me with the names of his favorite beers of the year. This was a formula for disaster.

I told Jill that she had to let go of past accounting with her ex. It no longer benefited her to recount past wrongs. I suggested that she wipe the slate clean. At first she looked astonished. How could she possibly erase all the terrible things her loser ex had done to make her life miserable? I told Jill to regard her past relationship with her ex as if she were a bookkeeper. Essentially, her ex had racked up so many debts on their relationship account that he qualified for bankruptcy. She'd be better off if she began an entirely new account column.

In reality, all relationships have pluses and minuses, debts and credits. Putting your ex's assets and liabilities down in writing is one way to help you see exactly whom you have for a parenting partner.

Exercise 5.5 Let Go of Debts and Transfer Credits

Get a piece of paper and draw a vertical line dividing it into two columns. Label one column "Debt" and the other column "Credit."

1. List all the wrongs that your ex has inflicted on you over the years in the "Debt" column.

2. List all the positive actions or gestures your ex has graced you with over the years in the "Credit" column.

3. Draw a line at the bottom of the list of your ex's negatives, or "debts." Underneath the line, write, "Account closed."

4. Draw a line at the bottom of the list of your ex's positives, or "credits." Underneath the line, write, "Transfer to account befriended."

Jot down what you learned from making your lists. Was the list of negatives longer or shorter than you thought it would be? Were you surprised to be able to write something positive about your ex in the "Credit" column?

What It Means to Accept Your Ex

Accepting your ex means you are willing to acknowledge the reality that your ex simply is the way he is. You want to focus exclusively on your ex's parenting style and skills. You need not approve of, or share his interests in, sporting events, vacations, or weekend activities. You need not approve of where she gets her hair and nails done, or how much money she spends. But you must accept your ex as a co-parent.

Accepting your ex means coming to terms with the difference between what you desire and what you have. Your ex may never be the person you would want, but nevertheless she is your co-parent. While you may wish to have a responsible, loving, and devoted co-parent, you may feel that your ex really doesn't fit that bill, and that's okay. You do need to have confidence that *you* will continue to be patient, compassionate, and generous, and that these qualities may nourish your ex and motivate her to be a like-minded person. You may need to gently remind your ex to always call you in an emergency involving the children; you may need to consistently tell your ex that you value her as a collaborator. And you may need to be compassionate with yourself that your ex has shortcomings and accept her for who she is.

Now is a good time to look back at the vision of befriending that you created when you began this book. Review what you wrote in your journal for exercise 1.3, "Three Steps to Begin Befriending." In that exercise you were asked to identify one small step you could take toward befriending. If you have met your goal, congratulate yourself! If you have been unable to meet the goal you set, see if you can understand what has been in your way. Either way, you may need to revise your vision of befriending.

Exercise 5.6 Revise Your Vision of Befriending

Take a few deep breaths. You have undoubtedly absorbed a lot of information about what a befriended relationship can be. Jot down some new ideas in your journal. Now, see if you can identify the next small step you need to take.

Conclusion

It's easy to get bogged down in old stories, negative feelings, and grievances. Keep in mind that in choosing to befriend your ex, you are creating a new role for yourself. Letting go of expressing inappropriate neediness and letting go of unhealthy feelings, such as anger, shame, and guilt, will help you develop an ongoing relationship with your ex, free of negativity from the past. Letting go is a muscle that you can develop and strengthen with practice. Holding on to the attributes of your ex that you would like to keep in your new, befriended relationship will help you develop trust that the two of you can work together.

In the next chapter you will see how crucial letting go is to befriending and how necessary letting go is to making an ally of your ex.

CHAPTER 6

the art of creating an ally from an opponent

"You know, doctor, I hate to say it, but Michael doesn't have a clue when it comes to raising children. He's so ridiculous: last Saturday night, the kids stayed over at his apartment, and he actually let Colin, our ten-year-old, stay up all night watching TV. He really doesn't know how to manage the kids or what to do with them. After all, I was the one who stayed home with the kids when they were little, so they're used to me, not him."

Sonia stopped talking and glared at me. They had been divorced for a year, and now Michael wanted to change the custody agreement. They were consulting me together.

Michael spoke up. "There she goes again, exaggerating! Colin wasn't watching TV; he was *reading*. How was I supposed to know I'd fall asleep and he'd stay up reading till 2:00 a.m.—which isn't all night!"

By now, Sonia was fuming. "It's just one reckless thing after another. Colin called me a couple of weeks ago from Michael's house. He wanted to know when his daddy was coming back. I was furious! These kids are too young to be left alone in the house." She turned to Michael. "When I tried to call your cell, you didn't pick up!" Sonia was close to tears. "Don't you understand what it means to be a responsible parent?"

"No one was hurt or scared—besides *you*, Sonia," he said, calmly. "You are overprotective." He turned to me. "These kids are ten and twelve. I was babysitting for my younger brother and sister when I was twelve, when my mom worked the late shift. What's the big deal?"

Sonia rushed on, bringing up more evidence of how unfit Michael was: He let the kids watch too much TV. He had a taste for whiskey. He was a slob. He never remembered what the kids liked to eat. And then her face dropped into her hands, and a sob escaped. "You are an idiot!" she shrieked. "And besides," she continued, again glaring at me, "how could anyone trust an unfaithful husband with children?"

In the moment before Michael responded, my heart went out to both of them. I could see visible pain on both of their faces.

Sonia and Michael were coping with a breakdown in trust. Sonia's distrust of Michael's parenting stemmed from, first, parenting-style differences and, second and most important, a deeper distrust of him because of his affair during their marriage. Michael didn't take Sonia's opinions seriously because he found her to be consistently critical of him and belittling toward his behaviors, attitudes, and relationship with their children. A breakdown in trust had driven these two parents farther and farther apart. Rebuilding trust is one of the common and major tasks faced by two people who have hurt and betrayed one another during their marriage.

In this chapter you will see how Sonia and Michael were able to convert an oppositional relationship to one of friendship, alliance, and support. You will find several exercises that will help you work on your own issues of trust. I introduce the concept of "limited trust" for those who are having an especially difficult time establishing trust with their exes. You will also find discussions and exercises to help you practice letting go and forgiving, and to set up guidelines for an alliance with your ex. You may move quickly through these steps, or you may need a long time with each step or certain steps before moving on. The order in which you do these steps will also vary. For some people, starting with the last step, "Creating Guidelines for Your New Relationship with Your Ex," works best. It probably took years to bring you to the point of divorce; your goal now is to achieve positive change consciously and expediently.

Identify Major League vs. Minor League Problems

In rebuilding trust after divorce, it's useful to differentiate between major league problems—past betrayals, lies, and deceptions—and minor league problems, which are usually differences in parenting styles that any two people, even people who are still married, might have. Major league issues are past hurts from your marriage or divorce that have left lingering negative emotions. These difficult feelings can make it harder to work out even minor conflicts. Even in successful marriages, minor league differences around parenting issues abound. Married couples are generally invested in finding compromises and keeping the peace, while divorced couples sometimes feel that they finally have a license to say what they *really* think.

Sonia and Michael were suffering from a major league problem (Michael's affair during their marriage), but were in conflict about minor league parenting problems (bedtime, whether it's okay to leave the kids alone). Often, parenting differences dissolve or are easier to handle once a major league problem has been identified and worked through emotionally. Just as often, battling exes mistake minor league problems, such as differences in parenting styles, for major league problems, such as betrayal. Don't get me wrong; life is all about negotiating and accepting minor league differences! And sometimes what one person sees as a minor league problem, someone else sees as a major league problem. But when unresolved major league problems persist, negotiating the simplest issues in day-to-day life can be impossible.

When Major League Problems Interfere with Trusting Your Ex

When I asked Sonia what was holding her back from trusting Michael, she had a hard time addressing only his behaviors with the children and, instead, continually referred to his sneaky behavior with "that woman." Several times, I reminded her that being a good parent isn't the same as being a good spouse. The turning point came when Sonia tearfully admitted that she couldn't get over her feelings of anger, betrayal, and hurt from Michael's affair. A major league problem needed to be addressed so that the minor league problems could be dealt with.

When Michael spoke, his voice cracked. "I really mean it, Sonia; I'm really sorry. And it's important that you know I love the boys, would do anything for them, and am committed to being the best parent I can be."

I asked Michael to say that to Sonia again. After Michael repeated himself, I asked Sonia to repeat what she'd just heard him say. I wanted to be sure she heard what I had heard: remorse, compassion, and empathy.

Sonia responded, "I heard you say you are committed to being the best parent you can be."

I asked Sonia, "Do you believe him? Do you believe he means it? Take a breath before answering." I wanted some time to pass to give her practice in reflecting and responding rather than reacting.

Tearfully, Sonia nodded. Her tears signaled me that his communication had gotten through to her. With this coaching process, Sonia and Michael learned to slow down, listen, and respond carefully instead of reacting. Michael expressed his remorse over the affair, acknowledged Sonia's hurt, and made a commitment in a way that she was able to hear. In addressing their major league problem, they saw their willingness to trust one another expand. Now they could move on to work through their minor league problems.

Just as Michael realized he had hurt Sonia with his affair, you may be aware of some deeper issues that you have with trusting or being trusted. The following exercise will help you figure out what holds you back from trusting your ex.

Exercise 6.1 Is a Major League Problem Preventing You from Trusting Your Ex?

Read the following list. Circle the number next to any of these major league problems that apply to your situation.

1. *My ex cheated on me during our marriage.*

2. *My ex was often unable to control his anger.*

3. *My ex was a chronic liar.*

4. *My ex was too absorbed in work to give me the attention I needed.*

5. *My ex had legal troubles.*

6. *My ex was a compulsive gambler.*

7. *My ex was an alcoholic.*

8. *My ex was a drug addict.*

9. *My ex was physically abusive toward me.*

10. *My ex was verbally abusive toward me.*

11. *My ex was unfair in our financial settlement.*

List in your journal any of these items that applies to your situation. Add any other issues you can think of that would fit into this list of major league problems that interfere with your ability to trust your ex.

It may surprise you to learn that even if you circled all of the numbers, you can still befriend your ex. Instead of getting angry about these major issues, allow yourself to breathe a sigh of relief. You are no longer married to your ex, and as long as this person is now able to behave as a responsible parent with the kids, then these characteristics are no longer your problem.

For example, if your ex abused alcohol or drugs during your marriage but is now rehabilitated, you need not dwell on the past, as long as you feel assured that alcohol and drugs are no longer a problem for your ex. If your ex's drinking, drug use, or gambling interferes with his current financial responsibilities, you will have to address this issue. If, however, your ex stays up playing poker until 3:00 a.m., but doesn't do it when the kids are around and it doesn't affect his ability to financially support the kids according to your mutual financial agreement, that's no longer your business.

Rebuilding trust with your ex will go much better if you follow the guidelines at the end of this chapter and learn to talk over your concerns with your ex (see "Dangerous Emotional Behaviors and Dynamics" in the following chapter).

Limited Trust

Even if you have been deeply hurt by your ex, this doesn't mean that your ex can't become a trustworthy co-parent and a valuable ally to you. Sonia may feel hurt by Michael's betrayal for a long time, and that's okay. The hurt doesn't have to disappear. You, too, may still feel past hurts. That's okay as long as you can mindfully and deliberately *set those hurts aside* in order to create a working relationship with your ex as parents of children who need and love you both. This is where *limited trust* comes in.

Limited trust is a unique way of rebuilding trust between exes after divorce, when there has been betrayal or damage that prevents the two from *completely* trusting one another. With limited trust, the trust between befriended exes is limited to specific areas, usually having to do with child rearing. What's more, it's okay if past issues remain unresolved. Sonia and Michael may never resolve the deeper reasons behind Michael's affair.

Differentiating between major and minor league problems is a useful concept for you to continue working on, because it will have innumerable applications to many aspects of your relationship with your ex. For example, you may be hurting from what you feel was an unfair financial settlement in the divorce. You may be upset that you settled for what now feels unjust. However, you may have to set aside that hurt from the past and focus on the current issues facing you that require limited trust: alimony, child support, and the innumerable ways that parents deal with money in postdivorce relationships.

Regardless of the extent of betrayal or hurt that you have experienced with your ex, in most cases, a trusting friendship of *some type* can be forged.

What It Looks and Feels Like to Trust Your Ex within Limits

Often, when a spouse betrayed you in the past, it can feel too dangerous to imagine trusting that person in the present. When I asked Sonia, "What would trusting Michael look and feel like?" she shrugged helplessly, so I asked her some more questions with the goal of rebuilding trust on a limited basis. I've modified these questions to address you, the reader:

- Can you imagine your ex picking up the children on time? Dropping them off on time?

- Can you imagine your ex helping your children with their homework? Supervising bedtime?

- How do you feel inside when you think of your ex being patient and loving with your children?

- Can you recall your ex giving your children swimming lessons, taking them to extracurricular activities, and so forth?

I wanted Sonia to focus on and remember some of Michael's genuine trustworthy qualities. Maybe the previous questions will help you do the same with your ex. You may also find the following exercise to be helpful.

Exercise 6.2 Practice Trusting Your Ex within Limits

Before going through the following steps, take a few deep breaths and relax (consider reviewing exercise 2.1, "Mindful Breathing"):

1. Allow three things to float to the surface of your mind that you currently trust your ex to do with your children; for example, *I trust my ex to drive safely.*

2. Write down these three things in your journal.

3. Notice what it feels like to trust your ex. Write a line or two about the experience of trusting your ex.

4. Now write down something that you would like to trust your ex to do with your children that currently is not part of your relationship.

5. What risks would you have to take to be more trusting of your ex in this situation? Jot down a few sentences.

6. Now take a look at what you wrote in response to steps 4 and 5.

7. Note in your journal how you might begin a conversation with your ex about this.

8. What do you want your ex to know about your concerns?

9. Be specific about your request. What exactly will you ask your ex for?

10. What would you need to hear from your ex to be a bit more trusting about this issue or item?

Of course, when your ex's behavior was far outside of what is acceptable, the major problem you had in the relationship might have been misjudging her character. I'm thinking of the woman who discovered that her husband had a secret life with dozens of call girls or the man whose wife flew into violent rages at the slightest provocation. Extreme personalities such as these do exist, but even in these cases, it's helpful to review the red flags and signs that you may have ignored in the beginning, to avoid getting into the same situation again. Full discussion of extreme personalities is beyond the scope of this book, but for further help, see *Impossible to Please* (Lavander and Cavaiola 2012), *The One-Way Relationship Workbook* (Lavander and Cavaiola 2010), and *Disarming the Narcissist* (Behary 2008).

What Prevents Your Ex from Trusting You

If you find yourself locked in the "blame game," believing that your ex is solely at fault for the breakdown of your marriage, one reason may be that you haven't yet looked closely enough at what was really going on in your marriage to recognize the role you played.

Recognizing Your Role in Your Old Relationship

Most of the time, as the saying goes, "It takes two to tango." Recognizing your role in the breakup of your marriage is crucial. For example, you may have to acknowledge that you failed to realize that you and your ex wanted different things out of life. Or, you may come face to face with the recognition that your anger was really out of control. Having the courage to look back and honestly come to terms with the role you played in the relationship dynamic will help you get rid of the residual anger that may manifest as blaming, resentment, or criticism toward your ex and that ultimately gets in the way of befriending. Another advantage to this process is that acknowledging your role in the breakdown of your marriage will better prepare you for success in your next relationship by making it less likely that you will repeat the same mistakes.

Exercise 6.3 Is a Major League Problem Keeping Your Ex from Trusting You?

Read the following list of untrustworthy behaviors that may interfere with your ex's ability to befriend you. Circle the number next to any of these major league problems that applies:

1. I cheated on my ex during our marriage.

2. I was often unable to control my anger.

3. I chronically lied.

4. I was too absorbed in my work to give my mate deserved attention.

5. I had legal troubles.

6. I was a compulsive gambler.

7. I was an alcoholic.

8. *I was a drug addict.*

9. *I was physically abusive toward my ex.*

10. *I was verbally abusive toward my ex.*

11. *I was unfair in our financial settlement.*

List in your journal any of the previous items that applies to your situation. Add any other major league problems you can think of to this list that might interfere with your ex's trusting you.

Even if you circled all of the previous statements, befriending is still an option. Just as befriending requires you to stretch in order to accept, forgive, and give your ex another chance, the same applies to your ex vis-à-vis your past behaviors. One difference is that it's not 100 percent up to you; all you can do now is initiate a dialogue expressing your remorse and asking for forgiveness (discussed later in this chapter).

Even if you have deeply hurt your ex with a major league problem, such as sexual infidelity or financial deceit, this doesn't mean you can't be a good co-parent and a valuable ally. Reestablishing even very limited trust, however, may take time, and a single apology or generous gesture on your part may not be enough. You will have to persist in reestablishing trust with your ex if the betrayal was deep. Don't expect your ex to immediately believe you are telling the truth if you have a history of lying. Nor can you expect your ex to deeply trust you with all aspects of his life or emotions. Perhaps the reestablished trust will be limited to a very small area at first; for example, your ex may trust you to return the children on time.

Shame

If the role you played in the end of your marriage was needlessly destructive, it would be normal for you to experience a lot of shame. It's important to acknowledge that shame. One of my clients, Gabe, had an extramarital affair shortly after his second child was born. When his wife, Deb, found out, she asked him to move out immediately, and soon after that, she filed for divorce. Gabe's affair lasted another six months. Two years later, Deb and he still haven't been able to rebuild even limited trust. They argue over little things, and he accuses her of turning the children against him.

Gabe's problem is that he harbors a lot of unacknowledged shame about having had an affair that essentially ended an already troubled marriage. It's easier for him to remain angry at Deb than admit he needed to boost his self-esteem with a woman fifteen years his junior. When he began the affair, Gabe had just been laid off from his job. At the time, he blamed himself for being unable to provide financially for his growing family. Plus, Deb was preoccupied with the new baby. He felt lonely and low.

Until Gabe can honestly acknowledge and cope with his shame, it's unlikely that he will be able to rebuild limited trust with Deb in the form of a new, befriended relationship. Shame is one of the hardest emotions to overcome. If you are dealing with shame, you will have to deal with not only the internal struggle of facing your own behaviors, but also the difficulty of facing someone you hurt. The following four steps can help you deal with your shame.

1. Take responsibility for your actions. No matter how driven or justified you felt at the time in doing what you did, nobody made you do it.

2. Don't blame your ex. The more you blame your partner for your own mistakes, the longer it will take her to forgive and trust you.

3. Don't shut your ex down. Be prepared to have more than one painful conversation about this.

4. Be empathetic with your ex. Keep in mind that your guilt and shame may make you feel uncomfortable with listening to how bad you've made your ex feel.

Expressing empathy, care, and concern toward your ex is critical. Showing that you are willing to bear your feelings of guilt, shame, or remorse without blaming or cutting off the conversation will go a long way in proving that you are worth trusting.

It can be difficult to come to terms with your role in the breakdown of your marriage, especially if the breakdown was due to a traumatic event. Recognizing the role you played in your old relationship may well involve shame. If you're having trouble with recognizing a part that you may have played, consider working on this with a therapist (see the guidelines in chapter 10).

Forgiveness

Along with limited trust, forgiveness involves a choice that you can make for your own well-being. When we offer forgiveness to a person who has hurt us in the past, we are replacing the artery-hardening power of anger with a softer, more flowing energy. When we ask for forgiveness, we are admitting our shame and vulnerability. Forgiveness reduces stress and increases optimism.

Forgiving Your Ex

Trust and forgiveness make befriending easier, but it's important to note that it's not necessary to forgive your ex for *past* injuries in order to trust your ex *now* in the matter of child-care issues. Divorce usually involves many disappointments that may be unrelated to your ex's capacity to be a loving parent. Forgiveness is a personal decision that has no timetable. Some people forgive early on in their postdivorce relationship and then go on to befriend, while others take much longer to forgive past hurts and are only able to do so after a reasonable and trustworthy postdivorce relationship has been established. Sometimes forgiveness just isn't possible at any stage. Even when a deeper trust that might require forgiveness of past transgressions isn't possible, it's often possible to trust your ex in terms of current child-rearing issues.

Exercise 6.4 Five Steps to Forgiving Your Ex

Here is a five-step model of forgiveness (Worthington 1998) that begins with remembering painful events. I am often asked why it's important to actively remember painful emotional events and whether it's necessary to remember pain to heal it, so I'll explain briefly.

When you have suffered emotional pain, you often develop damaging beliefs about yourself (for example, *I am bad, deficient, unworthy of love*). Remembering and processing painful events in a safe environment allows you to modify these core negative beliefs and develop compassion. You can do this exercise alone, or with a friend or a therapist. This is a lengthy process, and you will want to allot ample time, perhaps over a period of days, weeks, or even months, to complete it.

1. **Remember the hurt.** Take a few slow, calming breaths as you connect to the hurtful events you suffered in your marriage. Allow yourself to visualize some of these events in as much detail as you feel you can handle. You may find yourself crying with sorrow, shaking with fear, or tensing in anger. That's all fine. This step is likely to bring up strong emotions, so it can help to use your journal as a place to explore these events and the feelings they evoke. Allow yourself to know and feel your pain as thoroughly as possible. Allow yourself to feel the comfort you needed then and now.

2. **Empathize with your ex.** This may sound counterintuitive, but it's an essential part of the forgiveness process. Can you put yourself in your ex's shoes or imagine yourself as your ex's advocate? What do you know about your ex's personal history and family background that might have made him act in the ways that hurt you? Take a few more deep, slow, calming breaths, and try to feel your heart soften toward your ex. Even if all you can feel is a tiny sliver of empathy for one second, that's a start.

3. **Offer your ex the gift of forgiveness.** If you find that you can get to a place of forgiveness, you may be comfortable coming right out and telling your ex, "I forgive you for what you did that hurt me." Or you may feel more comfortable offering an olive branch: a tangible object such as a small

holiday gift or a token that has meaning to you both that will let your ex know you are offering forgiveness.

4. **Make your forgiveness public.** Often friends and family will follow your lead concerning how they should treat your ex. If you tell them, "I've forgiven Mary for her behavior and the ways she hurt me," they, too, will treat your ex with forgiveness. Telling other people will make your forgiveness more real and lasting.

5. **Hold on to the forgiveness.** Forgiveness is not a one-time act. Your hurtful or angry feelings may surface again, and you may need to repeat these steps. Each time you take yourself through it, the forgiveness process will be a little easier.

Forgiving Yourself

Once you have recognized the part you played in the breakdown of your marriage, it's important to forgive yourself. It's as unhealthy to continue to blame yourself as it is to forever blame your ex. People choose romantic partners for all sorts of reasons, and are motivated by all sorts of needs. If you can learn from your past mistakes, you will be doing better than most!

Forgiving yourself is a lot like forgiving your ex. Again, we will use a five-step model of forgiveness (Worthington 1998). What's important is to allow yourself to remember and feel the painful events with the goal of modifying any core negative beliefs about yourself. Processing painful events in a safe environment allows you to modify these core negative beliefs and develop compassion for yourself and others.

Exercise 6.5 Five Steps to Forgiving Yourself

Do this exercise alone, or with a friend or a therapist. Again, allot ample time, perhaps days, weeks, or months.

1. **Remember the hurt.** Take deep, slow, calming breaths as you remember hurting your ex. Visualize several hurtful events.

2. **Empathize with yourself.** Imagine yourself as your own best advocate. Review your personal history to understand what might have motivated you to act hurtfully. Take more deep, slow, calming breaths to feel your heart soften.

3. **Offer yourself the gift of forgiveness.** Tell yourself, *I forgive myself for being hurtful and contributing to ending my marriage. I am able to love, and I am worthy of love.*

4. **Make your forgiveness public.** Tell friends and family that you recognize and feel remorseful for the ways you contributed to the breakup of your marriage. Share with them that you wish you could change the past, but since that's impossible, the best you can do is forgive yourself and move on.

5. **Hold on to the forgiveness.** Forgiveness is not a one-time act. You may need to repeat these steps, and each time you do, the forgiveness process may be a little easier.

Resolving Your Issues

Michael and Sonia were willing and able to see a therapist who helped them resolve their issues around trust and develop a better relationship as co-parenting exes. They were able to listen to one another, understand one another's point of view, and, together, reach a resolution of their past and let it go. However, this is not always the case, especially in the early stage of divorce, when there are raw wounds. You and your ex may not be able to communicate on such an intimate level that you can resolve your unhealed wounds together. There may be a time when you might consider going to counseling together; if so, refer to the guidelines for choosing a therapist in chapter 10.

You may choose not to seek therapy at this time, and if so, you may trust that things will evolve positively in the future. Sometimes we need to rely on our intuition and good feelings.

On the other hand, you may never have the satisfaction of having your ex apologize, admit her past mistakes, or see your point of view. But that's okay. Hopefully, you have people to turn to: your friends and family will understand your point of view, and will be able to listen to you and empathize with your experience. Your postdivorce relationship with your ex will have its limitations, especially in the beginning. With time, the relationship may expand. When things get difficult, remember that divorce is not just between you and your ex; it's also about the children whom you share.

Creating Guidelines for Your New Relationship with Your Ex

The new relationship you will have with your ex will be, of course, much narrower than the relationship you had as a married couple. There will be many areas of your ex's life to which you are not privy, and the same goes for the access your ex has to your life.

The rest of this chapter offers practical guidelines and suggestions for handling the innumerable kinds of minor league issues that crop up in a relationship between befriended exes. If you find yourself dealing with chronic major league problems (for instance, alcoholism or poorly controlled anger) that might affect your ex's ability to parent effectively, consider consulting a therapist.

The Need to Change Your Reputation with One Another

Although Michael and Sonia had been divorced for over a year, they were still staunch opponents. They couldn't yet realize that when it came to the children, they were each other's best allies. Trying to right past wrongs or "settle a score" was a futile and exhausting task. To help them resolve their disputes, I told Michael and Sonia that they both had to change their reputations.

To Michael, I said, "Sonia needs reassurance that she can depend on you. Do you think you can really make sure that the kids get to bed on time? Can you remember to take your cell phone when you leave the house so that the kids can reach you if necessary? Can you be conscientious about picking up the kids when you say you will?"

To Sonia, I said, "Michael needs your respect. Can you give him another chance to prove that he's a reliable parent? Can you trust him to follow the parenting guidelines you've set up? Can you remind yourself that the kids are not in danger of real neglect or abuse?"

I explained that changing their reputations with one another would take time and that they could only do so through their actions in real time. It would require that both of them do some work on changing their behaviors and the ways they communicated. For the next six months, they came to my office to work through their specific fears, mistrust, and anxieties about each other's parenting. Gradually, they became allies. They came to see that although they differed in parenting styles, both had the children's best interests at heart. After a year, Sonia was convinced enough by Michael's changed behavior to agree to his demand for joint custody. What's more, the two now had a chance to befriend one another.

How to Change Your Reputation

Chances are you have a pretty good idea of what your ex finds objectionable or offensive about you. Should you try to alter everything about your personality to suit his complaints? No. You don't need to become neater (or messier), spend less (or more) time in the bathroom, or drive slower (or faster). But you do need to change your reputation in the areas that affect your relationship with your ex.

Graham had gotten into trouble by not paying his bills on time. To change his reputation, he needed to start making every child-support payment on time. Cindy had a history of problems with drinking and drugs. To change her reputation, it was her responsibility to get the help she needed to stay sober in the long term. Openly discussing with her ex the help she was getting gave him confidence and helped him build his trust in her.

Toni had carried on an affair during her marriage and had continually been unreliable, often lying to her spouse about her whereabouts. To change her reputation, she had to be scrupulous with the truth whenever she talked with her ex.

You may not agree with every demand for changed behavior your ex makes. For example, Michael didn't believe he had done anything wrong by leaving the children alone in the house. Unlike Sonia, he felt that a ten- and twelve-year-old were perfectly safe on their own. Instead of trying to convince her that she was wrong and he was right, Michael offered a compromise. He promised that if he left the kids alone in the house, he would consistently take his cell phone and let the kids know they could reach him. Sonia found this policy acceptable.

Exercise 6.6 Identify Your Behaviors That You Need to Change

Write down three to five areas where your ex has made it clear that she doesn't trust or approve of your behavior. Then number them in order according to how difficult these behaviors would be for you to change, with 1 being the easiest behavior for you to change. Then consider these questions:

1. What's the easiest behavior on your list to change? How can you change it?

2. What's the most difficult behavior on your list? How can you change it?

3. What behaviors are you unwilling to change? Is there a middle ground or a compromise that might be acceptable to both your ex and you?

The Power of Politeness

It may sound elementary, but politeness is a powerful method of communication. Politeness puts every event on a new footing, thereby giving you the capacity to dissipate the tension in your combative relationship. Politeness is often a wedge that can keep the door from closing between you and your ex.

By very definition, opponents do not harbor a great deal of trust in one another. And even people who are still in intimate relationships don't always prioritize tactfulness. This is precisely why it's important to focus, at least for a while, on the power of being polite. Now that you are no longer married to the person with whom you were once intimate, you have to step back and remember how to be tactful.

Like any relationship, separation and divorce have their own sensitive points. It's crucial to be polite to one another, especially if you are at the beginning of the important process of trying to turn an opponent into an ally. The following examples describe three common areas where politeness matters most.

Pickups and Drop-offs

If you agree to pick up the kids at 6:00 p.m. on Sunday, don't be there at 6:30 or even 5:30. Be there when you say you will. If you must change the time, give your ex as much warning as possible. If you expect to be delayed by even five minutes, make that call! Don't text unless you know your ex is more likely to pick up your text message than your e-mail. This is not only being polite to your parenting partner, but also being fair to the kids, who need consistency and reliability. In short, be where you say you'll be, or give a good reason why you're not there.

Schedule Changes

If you need to request a change in your child-care schedule for work or travel, do so as far ahead of time as possible. This communicates to your ex that his time is valuable and that you don't take it for granted. Pose your schedule change as a request rather than a demand. "I will be away on business from the fourteenth through the sixteenth, when Sam is usually with me. Can you take him during that time? If not, I will try to make other arrangements. And please know that you can ask the same of me in the future." That's far better than "I'll be away from the fourteenth through the sixteenth, so I'm dropping Sam off at your house at 5:00 p.m."

Eventually, when you and your ex-spouse are more comfortable in your postdivorce parenting relationship, you can loosen up and aim for more flexibility. Although it's always wise to be polite, your goal is to become more flexible with each other for the good of everyone in the family.

Child Support and Alimony

If you are experiencing financial hardship, such as difficulty making monthly payments, communicate this honestly to your ex-spouse, and do your best to pay your debts as soon as possible. Deadbeat parents are scorned not only because of the money they withhold, but also because they convey that they don't care what happens to their children and the other parent.

Creating Goodwill: The Power of the Present Moment

Creating goodwill and invoking the power of the present moment means you believe that people and their relationships really can change. Befriending your ex (and being befriended by her) means seizing opportunities for small actions that increase goodwill in the moment. Small, spontaneous gestures of help can carry a lot of weight. Creating goodwill is an excellent opportunity to take the high road and keep the big picture in mind.

The following are examples of clients who did just that: George, who had never been handy with domestic tasks during his marriage, sewed on the button that had fallen off his six-year-old daughter's jacket, which made his ex, Anna, realize that he really cared about pulling his weight as a parent. When Jocelyn requested a small loan from her ex, Rick, he readily agreed, as long as Jocelyn honored the repayment terms that he requested. Six months later, after Jocelyn had paid her debt, they both felt a deeper sense of trust. Marlene's furnace broke down one cold Friday in January, and she called her ex, Jim, to ask if their eight-year-old could spend the weekend at his house. When Jim responded, "And you're welcome to stay, too, in the spare room," Marlene felt, for the first time in years, that Jim cared about her.

The three couples in these examples have begun to create a reservoir of goodwill that each ex-partner can draw on in the future. In many ways, you can tap into your power to create goodwill in the present moment by simply acting decently and doing the right thing, just as you would do for a neighbor or any friend. This is letting go of an old divorce story where "beating up on" your ex was an acceptable way of life and the norm. It's choosing to travel the high road by expecting the best rather than the worst.

Exercise 6.7 Guidelines for Creating Goodwill

Many people start the day with a goal in mind, such as *Today I will eat healthily* or *Today I will make time to exercise*. You can add to your list *Today I will create goodwill*. Creating goodwill concerns being explicit about many ordinary things that might go unnoticed. Here are a few suggestions. Although they may seem minor, they are among the first steps to creating (and maintaining) goodwill.

- The power of "Thank you"

  I will thank my ex when he brings the children home on time.

  I will thank my ex when she returns my calls promptly.

  I will thank my ex when he remembers to bring the children's clothes and other belongings back to my house.

- The power of "Wow"

  I will let my ex know that the kids had a great time at her house.

  I will let my ex know that he did a great job.

  I will tell my ex how much I appreciate her help.

- The power of "Oops"

  I will apologize if I'm late.

  I will admit that I made a mistake if I bad-mouth my ex in front of the kids.

  I will try to do better next time.

- The power of "Please"

  I will ask for help when I need it.

  I will be tactful when asking my ex to change his behavior.

  I will return any favors I ask of my ex.

If Your Ex Does Not Reciprocate

Sometimes one parent is conscientious about being polite and offering small favors and goodwill, but the other parent doesn't reciprocate. Just as it takes two to fight, it takes two to befriend. If your ex continues to be oppositional and angry, there's not much you can do. Possibly your ex continues to fight with you because she is stuck in the past or feels closer to you in anger than in cooperation.

Here's the hard part: even if your ex doesn't take part in the "dance" that will transform your hostile interactions into a polite and compassionate relationship, that's no reason for you to cease behaving like an ally. Take the high road by sticking to your program, and you'll find that you can rest easier knowing that you have done your best to befriend your ex. And who knows? "Killing" your ex "with kindness" may eventually help her realize that befriending is far more beneficial than continuing to fight, blame, or antagonize.

Simple but Key Behaviors for Minor League Issues

Making an ally out of an opponent may take patience, time, and some finesse. Be persistent and take the high road by continuing to create goodwill and practice politeness—for the sake of your children. The remainder of this chapter offers practical guidelines and suggestions for handling the innumerable minor league issues that crop up in relationships between befriended exes. Again, if you find yourself dealing with chronic major league problems that might affect your ex's effectiveness at parenting (such as alcoholism or poorly controlled anger), consider consulting a therapist.

Keep your agreements. When you have made a promise to help your ex with a specific task, such as making a schedule change or meeting for some other purpose, do everything you can to keep your word. If there is a valid reason why you can't keep your promise, speak openly and honestly about it. Come to an alternative plan or agreement so that your ex is not left with unmet expectations.

Be consistent. This seems like a small matter, but it's huge in terms of building trust with your ex. Speak respectfully to your ex at all times, establish and stick to a child-care schedule, and generally behave consistently in your interactions. Do what you say you will do, and say what you will do.

Be considerate. Again, this is a rather simple tip, but one that's often neglected between co-parents. Letting your ex know about school events or doctor's visits, returning phone calls and e-mails promptly, and being flexible about your schedule whenever possible are the basis for rebuilding trust and working together for the sake of the kids.

Keep trying. Even though getting along with your ex can be difficult, don't give up. It's for the benefit of your children that you continue to make an effort to be civil with one another. Trust that in time, communication between you will get easier.

Listen. Learning to listen to one another without interrupting or automatically discounting each other's point of view is a key ingredient in any successful co-parenting relationship. Listen twice as much as you speak. Allowing your ex to feel "heard" can enable him to also hear and see your point of view, which helps you cultivate a mutual understanding. Listening doesn't signify approval, so disregard the fear that allowing your ex to voice his opinions will cause you to lose control of the situation.

Show restraint. Discipline yourself not to overreact to your ex, especially in front of your children. Realize that communicating with one another will be necessary for the duration of your children's entire childhoods, if not longer. Teach yourself to ignore those buttons your ex tries to push, and over time your ex will be forced to communicate in a more effective manner.

Ask for your ex's opinion. This is a simple technique that can effectively jump-start positive communications. Take an issue that you don't feel strongly about regarding your children and ask for your ex's input. For example, you might ask your ex for an opinion if one of the children is drinking too much apple juice or needs a change of bedtime. Allowing your ex to participate in the decision-making process on behalf of your children shows your ex that you trust her judgment and value her contribution.

Affirm your ex's relationship with your kids. Take a moment to tell your ex how impressed you are with his relationship with one of the children. Give him a genuine compliment. Acknowledge your ex's effectiveness as a parent. Saying this aloud to your ex can tear down years of defensiveness and anger.

Visualize a positive future. Visualization can be a powerful tool in creating the future you want for your children and yourself. Imagine a future where you and your ex can co-parent effectively, communicate clearly, and put the pain of your shared past behind you.

Conclusion

You can significantly facilitate rebuilding trust between you and your ex by identifying and working through the deeper hurt behind your distrust. Even when deeper hurts are not entirely resolved, just acknowledging their existence can prevent minor problems from escalating. Being mindfully focused on the present while practicing politeness, forgiveness, and compassion paves the path to befriending. Still, many of us experience pitfalls along the befriending journey.

The next chapter will help you identify and overcome some of the most common pitfalls that interfere with befriending: financial issues that mask deeper emotional issues, and problems that arise when you have to deal with the person who "broke up your marriage" but is still in your life.

CHAPTER 7

predictable pitfalls: what keeps exes enemies

Divorce is not a one-time event that ends with your signature on a piece of paper. Although that piece of paper defines a new legal relationship, the postdivorce emotional relationship is an ongoing process that is subject to constant changes as you, your children, and your ex grow. You and your ex may be divorced for longer than you were married! At different stages, befriending, as a relationship in process, is vulnerable to certain predictable pitfalls.

This chapter will discuss several pitfalls you may experience at different phases of befriending: dealing with dangerous emotional behaviors and dynamics, with resentment over finances, and with the person who "broke up" your marriage, as well as handling the desire to change your ex.

Dangerous Emotional Behaviors and Dynamics

Bonita and Corey consulted me two years after their divorce was finalized. Molly, their twelve-year-old daughter, had begun doing poorly in seventh grade. They were worried that Molly's poor performance reflected her difficulties with adjusting to living in two homes. I began by asking them about Molly, but within minutes they started yelling at each other.

Corey told me, "I know Bonita loves Molly, but Bonita is so irresponsible! When it comes to getting things done and being on time, she's a disaster!" Corey turned to Bonita and said in a mocking voice, "You think you could ever bring the kids back on time?" Then Corey told me, "Bonita is late every Sunday night!" Corey turned back to Bonita and said loudly, "What's the point of agreeing on a drop-off time? You never get there on time! That's what's making me and the kids crazy. You need to get it together! Should I get you a personal alarm clock? You give new meaning to the word 'late'!"

Bonita responded in an even louder voice, "Me, irresponsible? That's nothing compared to your messiness." She turned to me and said, "He's such a slob." She turned back to Corey and continued, "Don't you know how to operate the washing machine in that big new house of yours with every brand-new appliance imaginable?" Bonita turned back to me: "He's always been a slob. His mother told me that, but I didn't listen. My kids come home with every item of their clothing filthy; talk about irresponsible!"

Bonita stood up and began to walk out of the room. I suggested that she fight her impulse to withdraw and stick with our process. Begrudgingly, she agreed. I thanked her for her willingness to take a risk. It was time for me to speak up: "You two are giving me a taste of the tension your daughter lives with. I can see that you are having difficulties handling your differences."

I reminded this bickering couple that while they were no longer married, they still were communicating and would need to communicate for many years. I was guided in my intervention by the findings of family therapist John Gottman (1994), who found that learning to have what he called *productive disagreements* is crucial in any relationship. Bonita and Corey were exhibiting the four behaviors that Gottman (ibid.) identified as sabotaging productive communication:

- Criticism

- Contempt

- Defensiveness

- Stonewalling

Let's take a look at how Bonita and Corey resort to, and react to, these emotionally destructive behaviors. After the descriptions of each of these traits is information to help you identify areas where you or your ex may be engaging in destructive behaviors, along with suggestions concerning what each of you can do about it.

How Criticism Plays Out between Exes

According to Gottman (1994), a criticism is an attack on someone's overall character. When Corey says, "You're so irresponsible," he is criticizing Bonita by making a generalized attack on her character. Naturally, this makes Bonita feel hurt, defensive, and upset. Even if it's true that Bonita is irresponsible, it's unlikely that Corey's character attack will make Bonita change. Were Corey to say, "I'm upset that you bring the kids home late," he would be making a specific complaint about Bonita's *behavior* (ibid.), which she can then decide to correct.

Facing Up to Your Criticism of Your Ex

You may come across as being critical of your ex without your even being aware of it. Do any of these thoughts (Gottman 1994) ring true about your behavior toward your ex?

- *I get so mad that I can't hold back any of my thoughts and feelings, so I let my ex have it.*

- *I am compelled to blame my ex.*

- *My complaints usually begin with "You never" or "You always."*

- *It's easy for me to be coarse.*

- *Once I get going, I can't stop myself from piling on more complaints.*

Divorce can give people a false sense of permission that it's now okay to say whatever they felt for years but were keeping inside. An overly critical reaction to your ex may be a response to your own feelings of insecurity, anger, or pain. Finding fault with your ex can, in the short run, deflect from your own uncomfortable feelings about yourself. It can also deflect from your ability to get on with your own life. Blaming, fault-finding, and criticizing will only worsen problems between you and your ex. Here's what you can do about it:

- Learn to recognize the signals that you are about to go into criticism mode, and practice breathing, counting, or another strategy to defuse your emotions when you feel triggered.

- Make a commitment now to stick to specific complaints rather than launching an all-out attack.

- Remove blame from your comments.

- Stick with "I" statements (review chapter 2) and, rather than talk about your ex, focus on how you are feeling.

- Identify whether you are feeling angry and insecure.

Dealing with Your Ex's Criticism

You may be so habituated to your ex's criticism of you that you barely notice it. Do any of these thoughts (Gottman 1994) ring true about your ex's behavior toward you?

- *My ex lets me have it; he gets out of control.*

- *My ex has trouble sticking to one complaint and reminds me of all my shortcomings.*

- *My ex is too furious to express a complaint neutrally.*

- *My ex needs to complain to release bottled-up emotions.*

- *My ex lets unexpressed feelings build up to the point of explosion.*

Know that volatile criticism has no place in a befriended relationship and that you don't have to put up with it from your ex. Try not to take your ex's criticism personally. Here's what you can do:

- When you are about to engage with your ex in a situation where she tends to get critical, imagine that there's an invisible barrier between you and her comments.

- Treat the situation humorously: "Aren't you lucky we aren't married, and you don't have to put up with me every day!"

- Listen mindfully without responding to your ex's criticisms. Practice letting go.

- Ask if your ex has a specific complaint to make about your action or behavior. If your ex can verbalize a complaint rather than criticize you, listen carefully and respectfully.

- Tell your ex directly that you'd like her to stop criticizing you.

How Contempt Damages Your Relationship with Your Ex

Contempt is an open and deliberate sign of disrespect (Gottman 1994). When Corey asks Bonita if he should get her a "personal alarm clock," he is using so-called humor, or sarcasm, to tear her down. Other expressions of contempt include rolling your eyes, sneering, or simply verbally putting down your ex (ibid.). Contempt has no place in any genuine befriended relationship.

Acknowledging Your Contempt for Your Ex

Many people are reluctant to own their contempt for their exes. Do you recognize yourself in any of the following statements (Gottman 1994)?

- *I am often disgusted with my ex's attitudes.*

- *I can't help it, but I know I sneer and roll my eyes when my ex speaks.*

- *When one thing upsets me, I can go ballistic and insult my ex's entire personality.*

- *When I see my ex's faults, I just feel generally disapproving.*

- *Deep down, I don't respect my ex's actions or opinions.*

Contempt is often fueled by a lack of respect or admiration for the other person (ibid.). You may find it difficult to admire or respect the person you divorced, but your ex is still entitled to being treated with a modicum of respect by virtue of being the parent of your children. In time you may even come to admire your ex for his parenting or some other trait. Contempt will only harm the befriended relationship you are trying to develop with your ex. Here's what you can do:

- Learn to recognize when you are being sarcastic or rolling your eyes at your ex.

- Make a conscious decision to calm down using deep breathing when you anticipate that you will engage in this behavior.

- Lower your voice and slow down your delivery.

- Refrain from insulting your ex's personality; don't say "You're an idiot!" or "You jerk!"

- If you disagree with your ex, communicate directly rather than through nonverbal put-downs.

Dealing with Your Ex's Contempt for You

Recognizing your ex's contempt toward you may not be easy. Do any of these situations sound familiar (Gottman 1994)?

- *I have to ward off my ex's attacks.*

- *I feel unfairly picked on.*

- *I don't get credit for the positive things I do.*

- *My ex sneers at me and seems determined to find my faults over and over.*

- *My ex comes at me with insult after insult.*

Know that you are entitled to a basic level of respect in your interactions with your ex. If your ex was contemptuous during your marriage, let her know you will no longer tolerate being unfairly picked on or routinely insulted. Tell her that you would like to be friends and be able to solve problems together as they arise, but that you can't have a conversation if she is rolling her eyes or making sly innuendos about your faults. Here's what you can do about it:

- Identify your ex's behaviors as contemptuous, and disengage, reminding yourself, *It's not about me!*

- To disengage, breathe deeply and calm down. If necessary, leave the room for a few minutes to regain your equilibrium.

- Speaking in a soft, kind, firm voice, let your ex know: "This behavior isn't productive; let's see if we can calm down." Using "we" will make it less likely that your ex will get defensive at this suggestion.

- Be proud of yourself for using the pronoun "we" in the previous suggestion; it explicitly avoids blaming your ex, and is generous and kind.

How Defensiveness Sneaks into Relationships between Exes

Rather than tune in to what's being said, Bonita is defensive. Instead of listening to Corey's complaints about her lateness, she defends herself by attacking and identifying an annoying habit of his: bringing the kids home with dirty clothing. Meeting one complaint or criticism with another is a typical example of defensiveness. Other examples include denying responsibility and making excuses for your behavior. Adopting a defensive stance in the middle of conflict may be a natural response, but it doesn't help the relationship. A more productive response would be if Bonita could truly listen to what Corey says—without making a judgment.

Facing Up to Your Defensiveness toward Your Ex

Defending yourself is an innate reaction; it's a problem if it becomes your automatic response to your ex. Do you recognize yourself in any of these patterns (Gottman 1994)?

- *If my ex criticizes me for something, I have to set the record straight.*

- *When my ex blames me for something, I automatically deny it.*

- *If my ex blames me, I can't help bringing up everything he's ever done wrong.*

- *It's my automatic response to defend myself by focusing on my ex's faults.*

- *Sometimes things happen, like traffic! Why does my ex make such a big deal of everything?*

The first step in breaking out of defensiveness is to see your ex's words as information rather than an attack. Try to understand and empathize with your ex. This is admittedly hard to do when you feel under siege, but it *is* possible and its effects are miraculous. When a person is defensive, she often experiences a great deal of tension and has difficulty listening in a mindful way; by practicing *not* getting defensive, you will be better able to befriend your ex. Here's how you can do it:

- Train yourself to listen and say, "Let me think about what you are saying," rather than immediately insulting your ex in response to the things your ex says that make you feel defensive.

- Avoid saying "Yes, but..." (ibid.), which is the hallmark of defensiveness.

- Avoid repeating the same thing in a progressively louder voice.

Coping with Your Ex's Defensiveness

How often does your ex's defensiveness impair your ability to communicate freely? Do any of these thoughts (Gottman 1994) ring true?

- *Whenever I say something critical, my ex blames me for something else.*

- *My ex is a master at shifting responsibility onto me for something he does wrong.*

- *Instead of accepting responsibility for something simple, like being late, my ex retaliates and brings up my mistakes.*

- *When my ex makes a mistake, like being late with a check, she always blames it on external factors, like the mail. How stupid!*

- *My ex never apologizes or admits he has made a mistake.*

Defensiveness functions as protection for a person's insecurity. If you keep hammering at your defensive ex, she is likely to exhibit even more protection. Responding with defensive behavior or criticism ("You never want to talk about anything important!") is also ineffective. Listening and showing respect for your ex's experiences and feelings is key. If your ex feels understood and heard, then she is much more likely to break down her fortifications and engage in meaningful dialogue. Here's what you can do:

- Identify your ex as defensive, and remind yourself, *It's not about me.*

- Bring up issues when both of you are in a calm state of mind.

- When your ex shifts responsibility or blames you, redirect the discussion back to the issue.

- Ask your ex how he thinks the problem should be handled, and listen.

- Practice patience and compassion. Take a breath and start over.

- Walk away. Remember why you got divorced.

How Stonewalling Plays Out between Exes

Stonewalling happens between ex-spouses when a person withdraws and refuses to engage with her ex. When Bonita attempted to leave the session, she was stonewalling. People who stonewall simply walk out, withdraw, or refuse to respond by delivering the "silent treatment." Rather than blowing up, responding to your ex's aggression by letting her know that you are walking away is productive—but simply walking away from an argument without responding is stonewalling, which is unproductive. As a typical way of interacting, stonewalling during conflict is destructive to befriending. When you stonewall on a regular basis, you are pulling yourself out of the relationship rather than working out your problems. A more productive response is to stay with the emotions and do the difficult work of talking things out.

Facing Up to Your Stonewalling with Your Ex

Although, at times, walking away can have a positive impact, stonewalling is at odds with productive communication. Do you recognize yourself in any of these patterns (Gottman 1994)?

- *I usually walk out of the room when my ex picks a fight.*

- *I punish my ex by using the "silent treatment."*

- *If you don't have anything nice to say, why say anything at all?*

- *Conflict makes me feel physically ill.*

- *My family tradition is to avoid fighting. It's impolite to fight.*

People who are prone to stonewalling frequently regard themselves as neutral rather than disapproving (ibid.). Stonewalling can be a sign that you feel overwhelmed with emotions. It's important to realize that withdrawing during an argument is a hostile and powerful act. When you don't provide feedback through verbal interaction or even acknowledgment that the other person is speaking (for instance, by simply nodding your head), it's quite unnerving to the speaker and will likely make him feel even more upset. Here's what you can do differently:

- During a fight, when you are about to walk out, shut down, or withdraw, remind yourself to slow down and breathe.

- Take the risk of staying engaged in the situation even if your body tells you to leave or shut down.

- If staying engaged seems too difficult, say, "I want to talk about this, but I'm not ready yet."

- Later, after the conflict is over, reflect on how it felt to stay present when you wanted to leave. How was the conflict resolved when you stayed, as opposed to the times when you stonewalled or physically left? Write your reactions in your journal; answer the question: What is it like to stay?

- Tell your ex you can't stand being picked on and ask her to communicate differently when she yells or speaks in a way that makes you want to disengage. If she refuses, it may be a healthy choice for you to walk away, but first let your ex know you will continue the conversation when she can communicate in a way that's more comfortable for you. Speak softly.

Coping with Your Ex's Stonewalling

Preferring your ex's stonewalling over an explosive argument, you may have unconsciously encouraged this behavior without realizing its damaging effects. Do any of these thoughts (Gottman 1994) strike you as familiar?

- *My ex often tells me that withdrawing is better than being picked on.*

- *My ex refuses to stay in the room if I even raise my voice slightly.*

- *My ex purposely doesn't submit official documents by their deadline.*

- *My ex changes the subject or makes a joke when I want to talk about something he did that bothers me.*

- *My ex doesn't answer e-mails or phone calls about a problem I've raised.*

Dealing with an ex who stonewalls is frustrating. Your ex won't return your phone calls, or shuts down. Instead of saying she doesn't want to pay for your child's theater camp, she fails to turn in the required forms. Stonewalling as a behavioral tactic usually comes after prolonged criticism or defensiveness. Listen, step back, and wait for your ex to feel secure enough to break her silence. In practical matters such as the required camp forms, make sure you are the parent in charge of the paperwork. Here's what you can do:

- Recognize that your ex's stonewalling may be a reaction to feeling overwhelmed.

- Try saying, "I'm leaving this conversation now because you are stonewalling. Let's talk again when you can respond to me."

- Instead of nagging, criticizing, or raising your voice in an attempt to get through your ex's "brick wall," use "I" statements; for example, "I really need to talk to you, but I feel shut out. Can you give me a time when you will be able to talk?"

Strive for Productive Disagreements with Your Ex

Destructive emotional behaviors are often ingrained and habitual. In the heat of an argument, it's easy to get caught up in your emotions rather than be mindful. It takes patience and practice to change how you respond to a particularly annoying behavior or comment. Because these destructive ways of interacting are usually part of a long-standing dynamic, it may take time for your ex, too, to recognize the old ruts you fall into and develop new, more productive ways of interacting.

Disagreements and differences between you and your ex are an expected part of a healthy befriended relationship. Criticism, contempt, defensiveness, and stonewalling are behaviors that will sabotage your befriended relationship. Your goal is to identify when and where you or your ex engages in destructive behaviors, and to try to respond in the productive ways suggested in this chapter.

Resentment over Finances

Resentment over past or ongoing financial problems is one of the top issues that keep exes enemies. A lawyer friend once told me, "A good divorce is when both people think the other person got the better deal." However, feeling taken advantage of, ripped off, and cheated is a difficult thing to live with. And it's a difficult reality.

Yes, it's unfair if you put your spouse through school and then he asked for a divorce without so much as a thank-you. Yes, it's unfair if you are still paying child support even though your ex has a new, high-paying job—just because you agreed to a certain amount in your divorce settlement. It's unfair if both you and your ex trained hard for a profession, and the one who sacrificed career success to raise three children during the marriage now suffers financially. And yes, it's also unfair that women, on average, still make only seventy-seven cents for every dollar that men make (U.S. Department of Labor 2012). I can't dispense financial advice, but I can remind you that, indeed, a lot of life is unfair, and I can confirm that if you and your ex have conflicts over money, you are not alone.

Take the Financial High Road

Divorce is expensive. The reality is that two households are more expensive to operate than one. In addition, financial issues are an easy target for displaced psychological issues. Taking the financial high road means, above all, keeping your values clearly in the front of your mind. It means remembering that your children will suffer if they witness a lot of struggle over finances and feel that their expense is a cause of conflict and pain. They can easily feel guilty for causing strife between the people they love the most, their divorced parents. I recommend restricting your differences about the cost of raising your children to private conversations. Sometimes there's nothing you can do but swallow your angry feelings.

Taking the high road can assume many forms. It may mean putting your befriended relationship above money. It may mean putting generosity, compassion, and kindness above greed. Using the following affirmations may help remind you to take the financial high road rather than hold minor resentments concerning your ex:

- *Will this possibly matter to me in five years?*

- *I'm going to do what's best for the kids, and what's best for the kids is for me to grin and bear this.*

- *I'm not going to let my ex ruin my day over something so trivial!*

If you divorced through traditional litigation, you might have been encouraged to get the best financial deal for yourself. Yet this kind of thinking is not productive to a befriended relationship, where you naturally take the other person's needs and feelings into consideration. Taking the financial high road does *not* mean that you refuse to assert your needs and allow your ex to treat you like a doormat. In fact, the opposite is often true. By focusing on your befriended relationship rather than who has more or less money, you actually increase the odds that you both can feel as if you have "won."

Here are some examples of what taking the financial high road looks like:

> During divorce proceedings, Joyce chose not to fight her ex over who would get what part of their art collection, because she knew that, in addition to their monetary value, the paintings had greater sentimental value for her ex than for her. (For a time, he had painted seriously.) Several years later, when Joyce asked her ex for a loan, he remembered her consideration of his feelings during the divorce proceedings and was glad to oblige.

> Maria followed her attorney's advice to "get everything possible" from her ex. After the divorce, Maria found her ex very resistant to her befriending efforts. She felt his hostility simmering just below the surface. Three years later, when her ex was laid off, Maria offered to pick up all the expenses for the kids' summer

camps and after-school activities. She felt lucky to have a job that paid well. She felt even luckier when her ex softened toward her and they were able to have a genuine befriended relationship.

Bart and Carrie were both teachers with equivalent incomes when they divorced and created a binuclear family. Five years later Bart's parents died, and he inherited a great deal of money. He offered Carrie a small but generous "vacation fund" so that she would be able to take the kids traveling once a year. Carrie thanked Bart by giving him a photo album of their vacation so that he could see how fun it was for the kids.

Joyce, Maria, and Bart all took the financial high road by taking their exes' financial needs into consideration. They weighed their children's welfare and a congenial relationship with their exes alongside their own financial needs and wants. Taking the high road communicates that you take your own life seriously and that, down the road, you don't want to look back and cringe at how you managed yourself. The reality is that taking the high road generates personal benefits beyond the present moment. It's a commitment to emotional health.

Money Is Sometimes More Than Money

Finances are complicated. They are concrete, emotional, and symbolic. People act out all kinds of emotions via money: revenge, anger, and love are a few that come to mind. I've known affluent couples who fought over whether to spend five dollars more on a child's backpack, because the purchase symbolized one parent's need to feel that the child always had the best in the face of the other parent's fear of scarcity.

Here's an example of money's symbolic power:

When Jasmine walked into the apartment of her ex, Jim, and saw that he had a new couch, she felt a burst of anger and unthinkingly blurted out, "How can you be late every month on the child-care payments and keep telling me how poor you are, but be able to afford to buy a new couch? I'm going to start charging you interest for every day you're late with your payments."

Not until Jasmine got home did she realize why the sight of the new couch had set off such deep emotions. When they were married, she had always wanted to redecorate with new furniture, but Jim had never wanted to spend the money. Now that Jim had spent money on a couch (while simultaneously being late on child-care payments), Jasmine once again felt that her ex never wanted to give her the satisfaction of what she really desired. She realized she didn't care that much about Jim's new furniture. On a deep level, she was enraged because the couch underscored her feelings that her ex had never given her what she truly wanted.

Money and possessions have the emotional meaning that we assign them. If you can discover the deeper emotional meaning behind your financial resentments and tensions, you may be better able to recognize when a financial issue is "only money" and when it reflects deeper issues—power inequities, petty resentments, and so on. That realization can help clear the way to figure out when to take the high road and when genuine fairness is a reality.

Money and Children

If you want to be a responsible co-parent who puts your children's needs first, don't let your resentments or jealousies override your children's material or emotional needs—even when you feel that your ex behaves selfishly. This means remembering not to retaliate at the expense of your children. Be careful not to pit your child against your ex, even when you feel that your ex is taking the low road. Children want to believe that their parents love them, even when their parents are divorced. It's harmful for children to hear messages such as "Your father says he doesn't have the money—but who really knows!" or "Your mother is too cheap to give you that." This is damaging because when children think one parent is "good" and the other is "bad," they feel torn apart and must take sides—and taking sides involves losing one parent.

One of the most disturbing things I've witnessed is when one parent refuses to pay for a child's special celebration—a bar mitzvah, confirmation, graduation, sweet-sixteen party, or wedding—and the other parent (who resents footing the bill) "pays back" that parent by refusing to invite her to the event. Even if your ex hasn't contributed financially to your child's celebration, when you retaliate in this way, the person who suffers most is your child. Don't confuse what money can do, such as cover the celebration expenses, with what money *means*—in this case, who is generous and who is selfish. Keep in mind that your child deserves to have both parents be present at any special celebration.

Taking the high road means protecting your ex's relationship with the children in the way that you might have done had you stayed married. Stating the facts quietly is fine; for example, "After talking it over with your mother, I realize we really can't afford to get you a new computer right now." Regardless of how angry, bitter, or resentful you may be if your ex doesn't hold up his financial end, your job is to protect your children from feeling your anger and bitterness.

You and your ex will have to talk honestly about how much you each can afford and are willing to spend on your child. This can be tricky even between married parents. People can have vastly different opinions about how much is "right" to spend on housing, entertainment, education, and so on. The tighter the budget, the more difficult and charged these differences can be.

Let's look at the following example: Greg wants to enroll his thirteen-year-old son, Alfonso, in a special program for musically talented children, but his ex-wife, Elena, objects because she feels it's too expensive. Greg and Elena can argue for their separate positions, each accusing the other of being in the wrong, or they can do what befriended exes do: attempt to find a workable solution to the problem. Here are some of their options:

- Greg can pay 100 percent of the cost of special program.

- Greg can decide not to send Alfonso to the special program.

- Greg can ask Elena to contribute a percentage of the total cost, and he will pay the rest.

- Elena and Alfonso can apply for financial aid from the special program.

- Elena and Greg can find another special program that's less expensive.

- Alfonso can get an after-school dog-walking job to help pay for the program.

Children need and understand financial limits. But you and your ex have to try to come up with a workable solution if you have differences of opinion and ability concerning how much to spend.

Exercise 7.1 When Financial Issues Hold You Back from Befriending

Circle the number next to any of the following financial problems that applies to your situation:

1. My ex really screwed me financially in our divorce settlement.

2. My ex is chronically late or forgetful with payments.

3. My divorce agreement doesn't specify who pays for extras like camp or birthday parties, and my ex is unwilling to pay a cent for any extra activities.

4. I nudge the kids to give my ex presents, which I pay for, but my ex doesn't reciprocate.

5. Our agreement says that we share the cost of the children's clothing. My ex won't shop anywhere except at discount stores and my kids hate cheap stuff, so I wind up paying for almost all of their clothing.

6. My ex is more generous with the kids now than when we were married.

7. My ex expects me to chip in for expensive items that I can't afford.

8. After our divorce was settled, I discovered that my ex had bank accounts that I hadn't known about.

9. I settled for an unfair financial agreement in my divorce, because I couldn't afford expensive attorneys. Now I'm still angry that my ex has so much more than I do.

10. *It's not fair that my ex does things with our kids and their friends that I just can't afford.*

For each number that you circled, ask yourself:

- *Am I upset about the money or about something behind the money?*

- *What actions could I take that could make the problem better?*

- *What compromises can I suggest to my ex that could make the problem better?*

- *Am I taking the financial high road in this situation? If not, what would it mean to do so? Am I prepared to do so?*

Keep in mind that you always have choices: You can try to communicate your needs (review chapter 2). You may have to let go of resentment, bitterness, and destructive or unproductive emotions, and make deeper compromises than when you were married, for the sake of the children's well-being. Ask yourself what truly matters: financial equity or being friends with your ex. Because this is such a big step with the potential of disrupting a befriended relationship, you may want to seek professional advice before taking action.

The following are some of the issues that may arise when you are considering pursuing legal steps to attain financial equity.

Pursuing Financial Equity

It's all well and good to prioritize being friends with your ex when it's only your feelings or lifestyle that is at stake. There are times, however, when taking the financial high road with your ex is neither possible nor wise.

You believe your original settlement is truly unfair. When Nadine and Michael divorced, she got sole custody of their four children. Michael soon found a job that paid considerably more than the one he'd held at the time of their divorce. He figured that it was finally time to treat himself and his dates to the best restaurants in town. He bought himself a boat and a motorcycle. Meanwhile, Nadine was working full-time as a waitress and struggling to put food on the table. New clothes for the kids were a financial hardship.

When Michael came to pick up the kids for his Sunday afternoon with them, he waited outside the house. He and Nadine barely spoke. If they tried to talk to one another, an argument would soon erupt. Nadine had been brought up not to ask for favors and was therefore reluctant to ask Michael for more child support than their original divorce agreement stipulated.

When Nadine's waitressing hours were cut back, she finally decided to approach Michael. First, she made a list of her monthly expenses. Then she made a list of her monthly earnings and added the child-support payment. You didn't have to be a math whiz to calculate that she wasn't bringing in enough money to support the kids.

Next, she e-mailed these figures to Michael and asked if he could raise her monthly support check. Michael's response was to take the kids shopping for new bikes the next Sunday. Nadine thanked Michael for the gifts, but told him that new bikes were not a long-term solution to the kids' material needs. She repeated her request for more money in his monthly support check. In return, she got a nasty e-mail from Michael.

Nadine told her troubles to a friend, who recommended an attorney in town who occasionally worked pro bono. Nadine promptly made an appointment and learned that because their financial circumstances had changed since their divorce, there were legal measures that she could take to secure more child support from Michael. The attorney gave her the legal forms and advised Nadine on how to fill them out and what other papers were necessary. She told Nadine that if she needed more help, there were lawyers at the courthouse who were available three days a week.

It took some time and effort, but Nadine followed the necessary legal steps, and within several months, she was receiving adequate child-support checks from the state for amounts that had been deducted from Michael's paychecks. When Michael found out, he called Nadine, yelled curses at her, and told her what a terrible person she was. Nadine told him that she'd done what was fair for their children, and then she hung up the phone. At this point, pursuing financial equity was more important than befriending.

Here are some tips for pursuing financial equity when your ex is uncooperative:

1. Figure out your financial needs.

2. Contact your ex directly and ask for her financial support.

3. Talk to friends about your situation and seek advice from attorneys. Some kind of low-cost or free legal aid is available in most places. Most attorneys will speak briefly on the phone with you for no charge.

4. Persevere with the necessary legal steps. States have different protocols for figuring out what's fair for divorced parents with widely different incomes. If you can't afford an attorney, be prepared to do the paperwork yourself.

Your ex is resentful even though you believe your settlement was fair. In this situation, do some soul searching as you review the assets and expenses of both of you. Remember, mindful communication is key. If you feel that a new negotiation is appropriate, suggest that and see the following guidelines. If you sense that your ex is unwilling to yield the victim position and you continue to feel that your settlement was fair, remember that you don't have the power to change another person's feelings. The message to convey to your ex is "Even if you aren't happy with our financial situation, we need to co-parent to the best of our abilities." Accept that limited befriending may be all that's possible right now.

You realize you are benefiting at your ex's expense. Congratulations! Taking the high road seems to be intrinsic to your nature. You have the opportunity to right a wrong. Sit down with your ex and negotiate a new arrangement. Be prepared for several possible responses:

•   Your ex may thank you.

•   Your ex may unleash piled-up resentment.

•   You may have to renegotiate anew with your ex! Because the future is unknown, you may want to get professional advice to propose a new settlement.

When Either of You Still Sees the Person Who "Broke Up" Your Marriage

This issue can make or break a befriended relationship. If you can't find even a limited way to cope emotionally with the "other woman" or "other man," it will be truly difficult to befriend your ex. Keeping the big picture in mind—putting your children first by ensuring that they have two loving parents—can be especially challenging when your ex is still seeing or is married to the person with whom he cheated. You may have to work hard to keep your negative feelings quiet at family gatherings and tolerate differences between your ex's partner's parenting style and your own. The good news is that there's a lot you can do to protect your vulnerabilities and, at the same time, befriend your ex.

Learning to Set Clear Boundaries

One way to cope with pain and jealousy around your ex's "other woman" or "other man" is to set very clear boundaries about what you can and cannot handle. This will help you nurture and guard your own self-esteem. Clear boundaries will help you protect yourself from being exposed to situations and events that will make you feel sad, angry, or inadequate.

Ponder this question: *In what situations must I "endure" this person's company, and when can I let myself off the hook?* You can let your ex know that you are open to co-parenting, but are not comfortable socializing with a person who evokes discomfort. It's also important to clarify your feelings: the person your ex is with is not responsible for the breakup of your marriage; in fact, the person who betrayed you is your ex!

You are not required to be chummy with your ex's lover. Neil and Natasha had been married for ten years when Neil began an affair with Jule, divorced Natasha, and then married Jule. Neil and Natasha had school-age children they continued to actively co-parent. Six years after her divorce, this is what Natasha told me her life was like:

"I have as little to do with Jùle as possible. If she answers the door when I pick up the kids, I just say 'Hi' and 'Bye,' and that's about it. I've made it very clear that I'm not interested in talking with her or becoming friends. What happened between Neil and Jule still hurts. But Neil and I are friends again around the kids. He and I will go out for coffee if we need to talk."

I asked Natasha what kind of boundaries she sets concerning Jule's relationship with her kids, and she responded, "Jule is more formal than I am. She insists that the kids wear a clean shirt to dinner, even an outdoor barbecue. At first the kids used to complain to me about Jule, because they know I don't care about that stuff. I told them they have to follow Jule's rules when they are with her. I don't have much to do with what goes on at her house."

Boundaries may change over time. When an affair breaks up your marriage, initially you may not want your children to be around your ex's adulterous partner. However, it's unfair to your children to permanently object to the new partner, because that makes your children have to choose between you and the other parent.

> When Paulo found out his wife, Ingrid, was having an affair with his twelve-year-old daughter's violin teacher, Paulo fired the teacher. He justified this behavior as "creating a boundary" and protecting his daughter from that "no-good lowlife." Three months later, Ingrid filed for divorce. But a year later, after Ingrid married the violin teacher, Paulo realized that if he wanted to be friends again with Ingrid, he no longer could control when and how his daughter saw the violin teacher, who was now her stepfather.

A Renaming Activity

Do you have a negative nickname for your ex or the person with whom your ex cheated? Write it down ten times on a piece of paper. Then cross out the nickname, and substitute the person's real name each time. Do this every other day for a month.

Wanting Your Ex to Change

We all sometimes wish our exes could be different, but wanting your ex to change is a pitfall because it leads to trying to change your ex, which is an exercise in frustration. Let's face it: if you are divorced, you probably tried many times to change your ex's tendencies to be forgetful, pushy, and so on. Accepting what you can is preferable to persuading your ex to change. Being divorced means that you are no longer as affected by your ex's personality flaws and annoying habits, which we all have, yet befriending your ex won't make those particular shortcomings go away. You may feel that your ex drives too fast, spends too much money, makes too little money, neglects her health, spends too much time at the doctor's office—on and on it goes. Many of these issues are no longer your concern.

What *is* your concern is the subset of behaviors that directly affects your ex's parenting and your befriended relationship. Many of these behaviors you will also have to accept rather than try to change. Difficult as it may be, you may have no other choice than to accept these behaviors, especially if trying to change them would jeopardize the befriending process.

Here are some examples of ways in which you might want to change your ex:

- Your ex travels a lot, and you end up taking care of the kids more than he does.

- Your ex smokes.

- Your ex spends too much time watching TV with the kids.

- Your ex's new partner buys your children clothes that you feel are too expensive.

- Your ex takes the children on vacations you can't afford.

Each of these situations represents something you won't be able to change. You will need to step back or let go of wanting your ex to change.

Stepping Back Is Not Surrender

How do you manage to accept behavior by your ex that you might have previously thought was intolerable or that you disapprove of? The trick is to step back when you can. Stepping back basically means making a conscious decision to disengage from an unnecessary and probably damaging emotional explosion. Here are some ways you can do that:

- Assess. Is this topic something your ex and you are likely to be able to clear the air about, or will you probably have an argument? While it's always desirable to converse about differences, it's exhausting and unproductive to argue endlessly. If you think you will endlessly argue, you can choose to step back.

- Choose your battles. Ultimately you have to decide how important this issue is to you. You don't want to be anyone's doormat, yet there are times when you must ask yourself, *Is this the hill I'm willing to die on?* and if the answer is no, choose to step back.

- There's a difference between discussing an important issue and being the recipient of your ex's angry outbursts. Remind yourself that your ex's angry outbursts may be one reason why you divorced, and choose to protect yourself from toxic rage by stepping back.

- Remind yourself that you are two different people who see things differently and that you will have to disagree on this topic. Understanding this truth means you can choose to step back.

- Remind yourself that you don't need to be affirmed by your ex every time you assert yourself. Being affirmed by your ex is a need from which you can step back.

Exercise 7.2 Practice Stepping Back from an Argument

This exercise will offer you the opportunity to experiment with stepping back from an argument with your ex:

1. Imagine that your ex is being critical or nasty.

2. Anticipate your reaction.

3. Take three deep breaths.

4. Experiment with using each of the following techniques:

   Politely ask your ex to lower her voice

   Tell your ex you don't want to discuss this right now but will be available the next day

   Tell your ex he has overstepped your limits

5. Notice your internal reaction as you experiment with these techniques. Do you feel nervous, scared, or proud? Which technique felt most in sync? Write in your journal about your experience with this exercise. Commit to practicing "stepping back" once a day for the next week.

Exercise 7.3 Rehearse Ending an Argument Gracefully

Bear in mind that being nasty or critical toward your ex will only damage your befriended relationship and make your children suffer. Remember Gandhi's saying: "An eye for an eye makes the whole world blind."

1. Think of an argument that occurs repeatedly between you and your ex. Jot down a few lines about it in your journal.

2. For now it may be sufficient to memorize a line or two that will help you end the argument gracefully. The key here is not the exact words but your tone of voice and attitude. No blaming, mocking, or sarcasm allowed! You want to sound genuine and accepting. Here are some lines that have helped clients of mine end arguments gracefully:

   "Let's agree to disagree, okay?"

   "Can we take a short break from this?"

   "Help! Here we go again! We are getting into an old pattern. Let's not!"

3. Go back to your journal to see if any of these lines could help you gracefully end the argument you wrote about. If none of them is helpful, substitute your own lines. Remember, it's not what you say as much as how you say it. Attitude and tone often make more of an impact than the words themselves.

Inescapable Pitfalls

After their divorce, Miranda tried to befriend Joel. She was invariably polite and considerate, and shouldered the majority of the parenting and financial responsibilities for their teenage daughter. Yet Joel often ignored Miranda's e-mails and phone calls. He tended to cancel plans with their daughter at the last minute without apology or explanation. He was usually unavailable if Miranda was going out of town and needed him to look after their daughter. Communication was strained. If Miranda tried to reason with him, Joel became enraged and attacked her for things that had happened during their marriage. What's more, Miranda discovered that Joel had had an affair with, and was now dating, a woman who had once been a close friend. This woman was spreading bad rumors about Miranda to their mutual friends and even to Miranda's daughter.

Initially, Miranda was devastated. She felt hurt, betrayed, and angry. Joel's behavior felt mean and unfair. Still, she did not strike back. For the sake of their daughter, she tried to take the high road and be reasonable in dealing with her father. Yet after about a year, when Joel continued to be hostile and uncooperative, Miranda realized that befriending him was filled with inescapable pitfalls. She accepted the fact that their friendship was going to be very limited. She realized it was his problem, not hers. All she could do was let go, continue to take the high road, and keep the big picture in mind. Maybe someday they would be able to be friends, but she wasn't counting on it.

If you have tried continuously to befriend your ex according to the suggestions in this book and haven't noticed *any* change for the better in your relationship for at least one year, the pitfalls to your befriending are probably inescapable. If, despite your best efforts, your ex is making the relationship worse, and the pitfall is getting deeper rather than shallower, the sad truth is that it may be time to let go of the desire to befriend. You can only do your best in caring for your children, given the situation. Of course, if your ex is engaging in verbal, physical, or sexual abuse of your children or you, then there's no chance of befriending her until those behaviors stop.

Sometimes warring parents will ask me to define what is and isn't acceptable or right. Because every person has different comfort levels and standards, it's impossible for me to make that judgment. In these cases, I help the parents individually dig down deep to assess their core values and beliefs, so that they can avoid continuing old battles and power struggles. For example, most adults feel that parents doing drugs with their kids is an absolute no-no and, therefore, an inescapable pitfall. If you find that your ex is allowing your child to do drugs or engage in dangerous behavior, and your ex is resistant to exploring this issue, you may need to seek professional help. Sometimes seeking help with your ex is, in fact, what's called for. If you are interested, please see chapter 10 for guidelines for finding an appropriate professional.

The Only Person You Can Change Is Yourself

As mentioned before, to a certain extent, you can never change any person other than yourself. However, if you are in a committed intimate relationship, there's usually an understanding that each person will try to adapt to or accommodate the other. In a befriended relationship with your ex, you won't be processing your relationship as deeply or as often as you would if you were still together. Whether the issues between you are financial or emotional, or concern communication styles, it's pretty much up to you to make things better. If you and your ex decide to revisit old issues, you may choose to see a therapist (see the guidelines in chapter 10). It's important to remember that the only person you can change is yourself. You really only have control over your own attitudes and behaviors. And the good news is you *can* change yourself. Divorce can teach you a lot about how to do that.

Conclusion

This chapter has identified some of the predictable pitfalls you will face during the process of befriending your ex. Productive communication, which is crucial to befriending, is sabotaged by criticism, contempt, defensiveness, and stonewalling. It's critical that you accept reality and stretch into accepting the things you can't change, such as past financial inequalities and grudges against the "other man" or "other woman."

In the next chapter you will see how your life can become fuller, richer, and, yes, more expansive if you can overcome the pitfalls and allow yourself more joy as your clan expands.

CHAPTER 8

expanding the clan:
skills for making it work

Rene came into my office, upset. She was excited about her new boy-friend, Howard, but things were unraveling in her relationship with her daughter and her ex. Rene and her ex-husband, Rick, had separated ami-cably two years earlier, and twelve-year-old Mandy was coping well with their shared custody arrangement. Soccer was the center of Mandy's life, and Rene and Rick had been her avid fans. At first, Mandy welcomed Howard to her games, but suddenly she requested that he stop coming. Also, she didn't want her parents to show up together anymore.

Rene realized that Howard's arrival on the scene had disturbed the equilibrium she'd created with her ex. She wondered if the friendly rela-tionship that she and Rick had established was too confusing for Mandy now that they had both begun dating. Rene wondered if Mandy felt pro-tective of Rick, whose latest girlfriend had recently left him. To compli-cate matters even more, Rick's ex-girlfriend had a daughter on Mandy's team whom Mandy liked. As we talked, it became clear that Rene felt pressure from Howard, who wanted not only to attend Mandy's soccer games, but also, even more, to be included in Rene's life.

Rene wondered how to handle Mandy's requests. Telling Howard to stop going to the soccer games was sure to disappoint him. Being sensi-tive to her daughter was a priority, but acquiescing to Mandy's demands that her parents cease attending the games together didn't feel right; wasn't that giving Mandy an inappropriate amount of power over their lives?

In my work with divorcing parents, this kind of dilemma occurs often. Children may at one moment be fans of a specific arrangement, only to reverse their positions later on. Children can be upset when a parent's new partner unbalances the status quo between the exes. Befriended exes can normalize these situations by helping their children cope with the challenge of either parent's new partner.

Mandy's behavior is healthy: she is verbally expressing her feelings. Children need to know that they have a voice in family life when parents divorce. I suggested that Rene talk to Rick honestly about Mandy's new requests and her dilemmas. Rene found Rick to be a supportive sounding board. In the end, she decided to take the high road by putting her own desires (including her new boyfriend) on the back burner and honoring her commitment to her daughter's comfort.

Befriending New Partners: More Can Be Merrier—and Messier

Sooner or later, you or your ex may date, fall in love, cohabit, or remarry. You or your ex may even start a new family or acquire stepchildren. Although love and connection are reasons to be merrier, these changes also can make your befriended relationship with your ex messier.

Mindfulness, self-restraint, and solid communication skills will help you here. If you and your ex can talk through the rough spots with compassion and respect, practice managing your emotions, and be flexible enough to adapt to changes in each other's lives, you will find more reason for merriment. The bottom line is that you don't want to push the other parent out of the picture when a new partner comes into your life, and you don't want to feel pushed out by your ex's new partner.

Although the ideal situation in a divorce is for the two original (biological or adoptive) parents to remain the child's primary guardians and caretakers, that is by no means the only healthy solution. The following are some of the many possible variations:

When Don and Mara divorced, they shared custody of toddler Simon. Three years later, Don remarried. Soon after the wedding, the three adults decided that Simon would live with his father and stepmother, because his mother had returned to an acting career that entailed extensive travel.

When Ellen and Sylvie split up, they remained friendly co-parents of Sylvie's school-aged son until Sylvie partnered with Dana, at which point the three adults agreed to co-parent, an arrangement in which all three of them attended teacher conferences and medical appointments.

Jacqueline and Zach divorced in New York with shared custody of their two teenage sons. After Zach remarried and moved with his wife to California due to her work transfer, his elder son, a surfer, begged to accompany them. The younger son elected to stay with Jacqueline in New York. The family continued connecting harmoniously via VoIP (Internet phone).

Dates and Mates: Introductions

Whether introductions are mundane or monumental, formal or informal, they signify a new step in your befriended relationship with your ex. When you or your ex has a serious new partner, it's likely to rekindle old issues and bring up many new ones. Approaching this new stage of your life with intention and focus is important.

Introduction Dos and Don'ts

The following are two different examples of introducing a new partner to an ex. After you read them, I will ask you to write your impressions in your journal.

Denis doesn't peep a word to his ex about his new love interest. When his new girlfriend moves in, he's afraid that his ex will feel jealous and angry. He figures that sooner or later, his ex will find out and there's no use worrying her about it until then. One day, when his ex arrives to pick up their kids, she notices a pair of high heels in the hall. Just as Denis feared, she gets angry. He's surprised, however, that she's not angry about his having a new girlfriend—she's angry about the fact that he hadn't let her know what was going on in his life that would affect their children.

Valerie is quiet about her new love interest until things get serious enough that he is spending weekend time with her and the kids. That's when she calls her ex and explains that she is in a new relationship with a man named Mark. She compassionately explains that Mark might be there when her ex picks up the kids, and asks her ex how he feels about this. Her ex responds that he's not ready to meet Mark yet and asks if it's okay if he waits outside in the car for the kids. She agrees. By the following month, Valerie's ex feels comfortable enough to come in and have a cup of coffee with Mark before he takes the kids for the day.

In your journal, note which process is healthy and why. Which is unhealthy? Why? When, or if, you or your ex has a new partner, you will face new challenges and need new guidelines. Let's handle these situations one at a time.

When Your Ex Has a New Partner

Some divorced people have no issues when meeting an ex's new partner. I know a divorced woman who introduced her ex to a single friend and told them they were well suited for one another! More often, however, people do have difficulty when their exes have new partners. At best, you are coping with a change that you didn't initiate.

Coping with your difficult emotions. When your ex has a new partner, you may feel bombarded with difficult feelings; you may feel abandoned, usurped, jealous, or enraged. While these are normal feelings, you don't want them to sabotage the befriended relationship you have with your ex. For example, when Gwen fell in love soon after her divorce, her ex,

Jack, couldn't control his jealousy and resentment over the fact that Gwen's new boyfriend made twice what Jack made in a year. Jack hated going over to Gwen's house and seeing the lavish lifestyle she'd adopted with her new partner. It made him feel small and inadequate, as if he'd never been a good provider during their marriage.

It's perfectly normal to feel jealousy, resentment, grief, and other difficult emotions when you are faced with evidence that your ex-partner is moving on, but when you harbor these feelings, you hurt yourself and your befriended relationship. This is a good time to review the five steps for dealing with difficult emotions explained in chapter 2:

1. Recognize when you are feeling a difficult emotion.

2. Breathe into your emotions to calm down.

3. Name and befriend your emotions.

4. Accept your emotions.

5. Communicate effectively.

Tips for meeting your ex's new partner. You may want to keep the meeting light and short. Bear in mind that you don't have to like your ex's new partner or see her as a new best friend. But if your ex and, more important, your children have someone new in their lives, it's best for you, and for everyone, if you can meet and accept one another.

- Be aware that unexpected emotions may surface, such as grief, jealousy, and anger.

- Avoid making snap judgments about the new person.

- Your ex's new partner may be jealous of you! How do you cope? Breathe!

- Your ex's new partner may not like you! How do you cope? Breathe!

- If things seem awkward, it's okay to resort to small talk, such as weather and road conditions.

- Find a comfortable place to meet. Would you prefer an "adults only" meeting, or a casual meeting at a drop-off or pickup or while sitting in the bleachers at a soccer game?

- Call a friend afterward to process your emotions.

What if you're not ready? If you feel unready, give yourself permission to take your time. Perhaps you aren't interested in meeting anyone who is not in the "serious" category; if so, communicate your feelings gently and firmly. Or allow yourself a brief wave from the car when you pick up your children.

If time goes by and meeting your ex's new partner is still problematic (for example, it causes you to avoid going to family or school events), consider talking to a friend or even a therapist (see chapter 10 for guidelines).

Preparing to meet your ex's new partner's children. When and if your ex's new partner introduces his children to yours, your sense of loss may extend even further. The people, values, and activities in your ex's new world may affect your kids in ways that make you uncomfortable. A new round of difficult feelings of competition, jealousy, and loss may be evoked. You will best cope with this situation if you strengthen your ability to center yourself and regulate your emotions.

When You Have a New Partner

Don't be surprised if your ex has a difficult time adjusting to your new partner. Although sometimes it may be tempting to write off the friendship with your ex at this point if things feel too difficult, it's in everyone's best interest if you and your ex can weather this transition.

Integrating your new partner into your family life may take longer and be more complicated than you imagined. If you and your ex are close co-parents, your new partner will eventually have to relate to your ex. This relationship can range from polite and cordial to a collaboration around the myriad of child-rearing issues.

Many divorced parents feel more comfortable dating only when the children are with their other parent. Although this can be a workable short-term solution and, indeed, may be a good arrangement in the beginning of your new relationship, eventually, if you're building a serious relationship, your new love interest becomes a partner who is integrated into your family life. The good news is that once the initial awkwardness is overcome, I have seen how, again and again, the ex and the new partner become friendly, and sometimes even become friends. I know of divorced couples where the ex comes over to watch football games with the new husband and all the kids. Keep in mind that you have many options and choices as to how far and how fast to integrate your new partner into your family life.

Introducing your new partner to your ex. When and how you introduce a new partner to your ex is a major step in expanding the clan, and it's best if everyone begins on good footing. Even if a new partner doesn't become permanent, it's wise to set a positive precedent for how you and your ex will handle the new people in each other's lives. Develop compassion for your ex, your new partner, and yourself at this important juncture. Reread the "Tips for Meeting Your Ex's New Partner" presented earlier in the chapter, and add the following:

- Tell your ex directly that you want to introduce your new partner.

- Ask your ex how she feels about this introduction.

- Honor your ex's feelings, whatever they are.

- Remember, there's no right or wrong about the timing of an introduction.

- If the introduction doesn't go smoothly, don't despair. There's always the next time.

If your children have already met your new partner, it's a good idea to mention it to your ex. Communicate and keep what's happening out in the open. Don't make the children be the messengers or secret keepers.

Coping with your ex's difficult behaviors concerning your new partner. Do any of these situations sound familiar?

- "My ex wouldn't come to Sarah's school play because my boyfriend was going to be there."

- "My ex refuses to say hello to my girlfriend when she drops off the kids."

- "My ex stopped talking to me ever since I came out as gay and my lover moved in."

- "My ex refers to my partner as 'the slut.'"

If one of these situations resonates with you, first speak calmly with your ex and let him know you feel that his behavior is hurtful and inappropriate, and that you hope he can be mature enough to behave politely. Ask if there is anything you are doing that makes your ex feel uncomfortable.

> Lina learned that her ex felt very uncomfortable whenever he saw her new partner, Joey, with his arm around her. Her ex admitted that although it was "irrational," he felt jealous and angry. Lina was willing to accommodate her ex and ask Joey to be less demonstrably affectionate when her ex was around.

However, the reality is that you cannot force your ex to be pleasant. If your ex is rude or nasty to your new partner, the behavior may well stem from your ex's difficult emotions, but the emotions are not within your control to fix or change.

Can you think of a time when your ex slighted or insulted your partner? If you haven't begun dating, have you ever felt a sense of dread when you imagine introducing your ex to a new partner? Keep in mind that regardless of your ex's behavior, you will cope best with this situation if you strengthen your ability to center yourself and regulate your emotions. Again, take a look at the five-step process in chapter 2 and review the exercises from chapters 3 and 4.

Sometimes your ex may make a request or demand that seems unreasonable to you. Your ex may refuse to attend a family event if you bring your new partner. Your ex may be furious that you introduced a new dating partner to the children first. There's no one-size-fits-all answer for the multitude of situations that arise in postdivorce life involving dating and expanding the clan. It's always important for you to:

- Talk through each situation and look for a compromise that keeps the best interest of the children in the forefront of the picture.

- Take responsibility for your own behaviors.

- Take responsibility for your own reactions to your ex's behaviors and demands.

Remember to respond rather than react. You may want to review chapter 4, which focuses on how you can be responsive rather than reactive. Here's a helpful exercise (Goldstein 2012) that's easy to remember and can help you brush up on that skill.

Exercise 8.1 STOP

When you fear losing control of your emotions with your ex, practice these four steps:

1. S = Stop.

2. T = Take a breath.

3. O = Observe your body.

4. P = Pause and ask yourself, *What can I do to calm down?*

When your ex doesn't accept your new partner. Your ex may manifest a host of behaviors that feel antagonistic, rude, or nasty to you or your partner. These behaviors undoubtedly come from your ex's inner issues; perhaps she feels lonely, resentful, or jealous. Here's what you need to know and do:

- **Your ex must own and face her own emotions.** You are not your ex's therapist or best friend. If your ex tells you with his words or actions that he is upset about your new partner, you can say, "I'm sorry this is difficult for you." While it's tempting to get into long conversations, or to try to comfort your ex or minimize the importance of your new relationship, these kinds of conversations are usually not productive.

- **Speak compassionately to your ex about what's bothering her.** Before starting a stressful conversation with your ex, tap into your own compassion. Take a few deep breaths, think about your ex, and remind yourself:

  Just like me, my ex wants to have a happy postdivorce life.

  Just like me, my ex was hurt by the past in our marriage.

  Just like me, my ex wants to have a befriended relationship.

  Just like me, my ex wants to be close to our children.

- **Set boundaries with compassion.** Find a time when you and your ex can speak quietly. Look your ex in the eye and state very clearly what is and isn't acceptable, and what kind of consequences your ex can expect if he continues his behavior.

Tara told her ex, "It's not acceptable for you to be rude to my new partner. If you continue to do so, I will not invite you into my house." Jed told his ex, "It's not acceptable for you to just walk into my house without letting me know in advance. If you continue to do so, I will ask you for your key."

Your goal is to set boundaries such that your ex will modify behaviors that would otherwise harm your relationship with a new partner.

Parenting with Your Ex When the Clan Expands

Most children harbor fantasies of their "real" parents getting back together, and when a parent has a new partner, that possibility seems less likely. Children often feel jealous of a parent's new partner after having had that parent all to themselves for a while. Although it's beyond the scope of this book to discuss the many and varied factors that affect how children adjust to a parent's new partner or a stepparent, innumerable books abound on this subject. (See for instance *The Divorce Workbook for Children* [2008] and *The Divorce Workbook for Teens* [2008].) Keep in mind that your job is to cooperate and communicate with your ex to best help your children through the transition as the clan expands.

Keep Your Ex in the Loop

If you have a new partner, make sure to keep your ex in the loop about the children's schedules, events, health, and emotional well-being. No matter what relationship your children develop with your new partner—close, distant, stormy, loving—your ex is still your child's unique father or mother, and deserves a permanent and special place in your child's life. Regardless of who you are dating or married to, your job is to support your ex in being a loving and involved parent. Your ex should be included in all major child celebrations and milestones, such as birthdays, graduations, weddings, and even some minor events, such as school performances or athletic events.

If your ex has a new partner, it is your right and obligation to be in the loop about the children's physical and emotional well-being, and involved in their day-to-day events and schedules. Let your ex know that you need to be kept informed about any and all details of your child's life. However, don't rely solely on your ex for information. Ask the other adults in your child's life—teachers, doctors, coaches, camp counselors—to include you in e-mails, phone trees, mailings, and meetings. These professionals may be new to working with divorced parents or may need your input for something as simple as sending out information to two parents at different addresses.

• Mom's House, Dad's House

Shane and Nora were doing a good job of co-parenting their eleven-year-old son until Nora began dating Hernandez, whose three children were technology geeks. Hernandez's children liked to make stop-animation movies and mess around with their computers. Now, when Nora and Hernandez were together with their shared children, the highlight of the weekend was a trip to the computer store.

Shane was upset that his son was spending every weekend indoors. He believed that weekends are for outdoor activity. Once, Nora believed that, too. Fortunately, Shane was able to discuss his feelings with Nora. She told him she didn't mind the change in activities, because her main focus was whether their son would get along with Hernandez's kids. But she acknowledged Shane's concern. As they talked further, Shane accepted that their son would do outdoor activities on weekends when he was at his house but that Nora decided on weekend activities when their son was at her house. Nora realized she missed being outdoors and, the next weekend with Hernandez, suggested they all take an adventure trip to the woods.

This story has a happy ending. Shane and Nora were able to talk openly and honestly to one another, acknowledge their differences, and come up with a workable solution. They also observed the unwritten rule of binuclear families: parents set the rules and activities at their own houses, but generally don't interfere with what happens at the other parent's house unless safety is violated.

Bear in mind that although children can adapt to two different parenting styles and situations, the more consistent that parents make their individual households and the less strife between the exes, the easier it will be for the children and the befriended relationship.

New partners often introduce new ways of being that can cause conflict between you and your ex, and that's a good time to discuss modifications to co-parenting arrangements. Shane and Nora's differences were about how their child spent his weekends. These same issues pertain to a new partner who, for example, introduces to the household a new religious observance, a new cultural context, a new diet, or new discipline methods.

Especially Sticky Situations: When Children Suffer

Some situations are inherently stickier than others for befriending. One especially sticky situation is when your children complain profoundly about your ex's new partner. This situation is even more difficult if your ex's new partner has children and your children are resentful toward the partner *and* her children. It's still more difficult if your ex's new partner is "the person who broke up the marriage," and now your children complain about the partner as well as her children and family.

Many children complain about a parent's new partner. Depending on their temperament and developmental stage, children are more or less receptive to this new person in their lives. Your children may complain about both your new partner and your ex's, and in this case, befriended exes often find themselves commiserating with one another!

Let your child know that adjusting to new people is often difficult. While complaints such as "I don't like the perfume Dad's new girlfriend wears" or "Mom's new boyfriend isn't very smart" don't sound very serious, you do need to take your child's complaints seriously. They may simply reflect the grief and disappointment that comes with accepting that their original family is gone. They may feel as if they would be disloyal to you if they accepted your ex's new partner. On the other hand, their complaints may reflect something more important, such as feeling neglected or even abused, as the clan expands. How do you distinguish between normal complaints and truly harmful situations?

Develop a matter-of-fact way of asking simple, noninvasive questions; for example: "What movie did you see with Dad and his new friend?" "Did Mom's boyfriend cook something you liked?" By asking these questions, you let your child know it's safe to talk about your ex's new partner.

If your child has a complaint, adopt a tone between matter-of-fact and serious that allows you to explore what's really bothering your child. "She's so mean" or "He's so strict" may mask the desire for parents to reunite, or it may have some justification.

Listen carefully and patiently. Let your child know that his feelings matter. Encourage your child to relate all the details, and ask for specific incidents. Questions to ask might include: "Give me an example of how she spoke to you" and "Did this happen more than once?"

Listen for the underlying, unspoken feelings your child may be trying to express. Listen with compassion and empathy, by mirroring what's being said to you and checking in: "Am I getting what you are telling me?" Gently remind your child that you and your ex are divorced, that your child's well-being is a top priority, and that you don't want to see your child upset. Be specific and remind your child, "If Mommy's new boyfriend says or does anything that hurts your feelings, please tell Mommy, or if you are afraid to tell her, tell me. If anyone, including Mommy's new boyfriend, hurts you physically, that's not acceptable, and you must tell me right away!"

Suggest that your child speak directly to your ex. Offer to be part of the conversation if it will make your child more comfortable: "Can you tell Daddy that his girlfriend hurt your feelings?" "Do you want me to be there when you tell Mommy that her new friend asks too many questions and that sometimes you just want to be alone in your room?"

If your child is reluctant to talk directly to your ex, get the child's permission and relay the information to your ex. Present your child's complaint as carefully, gently, and neutrally as possible. Try to understand your ex's perspective.

Check in with your own attitudes toward your ex's new partner. Children pick up on parents' feelings. If you dislike your ex's new partner, it's possible that your child is acting on your behalf. Your job is to help your child adjust to this new situation. Be honest and admit your own feelings while encouraging your child to adjust; for example, "I liked Dad's old girlfriend better than Sally too, but you and I don't get to choose. Your job is to have as much fun as you can when you are at Dad's. How can I help you?"

If your child displays continued anxiety or depression, is failing in school, is abusing alcohol or drugs, or is getting into trouble with the law, sit down and discuss calmly with your ex the possibility of seeking professional help. Now is the time to act. It's easier to help a child or teenager who is having trouble before the problems expand than to treat that same person as an adult who is in serious, long-term trouble. Your child's school counselor or pediatrician is a good person to consult.

Finally, if at any time, you become suspicious that your child is being physically, sexually, or emotionally abused by your ex or your ex's partner, you need to take immediate action and prohibit your child from staying at your ex's house. Seeking professional assistance in such situations is highly recommended.

Conclusion

In this chapter you've explored many issues that you may face as the clan expands. You've learned some new skills to help you at this stage of your journey. Remember, it's not unusual for it to take years before your children, your ex, and you become comfortable with all of the new roles and relationships in an expanded clan. Be patient: evolving clans take time, patience, and lots of communication! Over time and with practice, you may develop a new kind of balance that allows you to enjoy a holiday table that's full of people you might never have thought it possible to befriend. I will address this topic in the next chapter: how rituals and celebrations are opportunities for transformation.

CHAPTER 9

rituals and celebrations as transformative opportunities

Remember Helena, from chapter 1, who celebrated Thanksgiving with her expanded clan? The following scenes from Helena's Thanksgiving will give you an idea of what it looks like when befriended exes who have formed a binuclear family gather for a holiday.

It's 8:30 a.m., and Helena has just put a thirty-pound turkey in the oven. Brian, aged nine, and his stepsister Julia, five, are making decorative placards for the guests who will be gathering in a few hours around the big dining room table. As they color, the children discuss how they are related to the guests. Julia knows that Joel is her dad and Brian's dad; that Helena is her mom; that Lynn is Brian's mom; and that Granny Sheila is Helena's mom. But she's stumped by some of the other names.

Older brother Brian explains, "Tony is my mom's new husband, and Jonah is Tony's son, who goes to college. And Robbie is your mom's old husband." Helena smiles as she hears the children talking. "Why is Robbie old?" Julia asks. Helena answers, "Robbie isn't really old; he's exactly my age. He's my ex-husband. And we're all still family."

There are other people invited, too: not only Helena's sister and brother-in-law, and their children, but also Helena's sister-in-law from her first marriage. They are truly an expanded clan. This is the first time so many people are coming to Thanksgiving, and Helena is a little nervous about how everyone will get along.

The holiday celebration turns out to be festive and a lot of fun. What makes this possible is that Joel has befriended his ex, Lynn, and Helena has befriended her ex, Robbie. Of course, it hasn't always been this way, and over the years, everyone has done some hard relational work. From the outside, though, the gathering looks like any other extended family celebrating a holiday.

Later, when Helena and her sister are in the kitchen, cleaning up after the meal, Helena's sister says, "There's something wrong with this picture: you got divorced and now have the big family, but I'm married to my children's father and I have a small family!" Helena's eyes fill with tears as she remembers the pain of the dissolution of her first marriage. "You know, I would never recommend divorce as a route to having a big family." But she feels thankful for all the love in the house this special day.

Take a moment to absorb the huge number of transitions this family story reflects. Helena and Joel have now been married for seven years. Each was previously married; parented children in the former marriage; navigated the pain and difficulty of divorce and being newly single; and finally met and married the other. And thus began the next phase of their work: the befriending of their exes, which culminated in this joyous Thanksgiving.

No matter where you are on the spectrum of separation, divorce, and befriending—whether you are just beginning to think about separation or have been divorced for many years—this chapter will give you some important ideas about how you can move into a more befriended relationship.

Divorce Rituals as Harbingers of Befriending

Throughout time, rituals have marked significant moments and transitions in the life cycle. Rituals and ceremonies are powerful ways to honor important moments such as birth, marriage, and death. Other rituals mark significant milestones, celebrating adulthood (bar mitzvah and sweet sixteen) and graduation. Holidays such as Thanksgiving, Christmas, and the Fourth of July are another kind of ritual. My working definition of a *ritual* is a set of actions set apart from ordinary time that are done with intention and that have meaning to *you*.

For most people, signing the divorce papers is their default divorce ritual. In the last twenty years, as divorce has become less shameful, new rituals have sprung up to commemorate the significance and importance of divorce. Yet very few of these ceremonies emphasize befriending, because it's only over time that you can really begin to wrap your head around the ways in which your life is still intertwined with your ex and will forever be. Although it's usually unrealistic to think of being good friends with your ex right off the bat, you can create rituals that will increase your chances of becoming friends at some future date, by emphasizing goodwill and doing the least harm.

Divorce rituals that emphasize befriending can be a one-time event to mark, for example, the end of your marriage, or they can be repeated occurrences, for example, marking the Sunday night when the kids switch from one parent's house to the other's. Rituals create, sustain, and reinforce the idea that divorce doesn't have to be destructive, and they acknowledge both the children's and the parents' need to heal from the inevitable suffering. The following are some examples.

> Laurel and Todd took a quiet walk by the nearby river with their children after telling them about their separation. Their intention was to let the children know that they could still be together as a family and participate in things they previously enjoyed together. Laurel suggested they all throw stones into the moving water, and Todd talked about how although the river kept moving and changing, it was still a river.

Shortly after she and Denny announced their divorce to the children, Ilana created an altar on the mantle with a photo and candle for each family member. The parents and their three children lit the candles and silently watched them burn down as Ilana explained that it was okay to feel sad that one part of their life was ending, but to remember that they would still belong to the family in the next part of their life. Ilana had also placed an empty, open box on the altar, which she told the children symbolized openness to the new space they would inhabit in the future.

Andrea and Andrew wrote down what they honored about their years together and then read them aloud to each other. Andrew read, "I honor the births of our two wonderful children," and Andrea read, "I honor how hard we tried to make things work." At the conclusion of the readings, they returned their wedding rings to each other. After the ceremony, each left with respective family and friends to gather somewhere private (as people do after a funeral or wake), where grieving would be supported.

When Cecil moved to a new house after he and his wife of fourteen years split up, he invited both his and her parents, siblings, and a few good friends to join him, his ex, and their children for brunch. The "housewarming" marked the end of one phase of his life and the beginning of the next. After everyone gathered, he guided them in a candle-lighting ceremony: each person, including his ex-wife, lit a candle and placed it on a tray one of his children had made in camp. With all the candles lit, he stated that the purpose of the event was to remind everyone, especially his children, that they were all still family. He then said the Lord's Prayer, and the guests shared in a delicious meal.

Some people even feel that divorce is an occasion to celebrate. Divorced after less than three years of marriage, Manhattanites Charles Bronfman and his ex-wife, Bonnie, invited one hundred of their friends to an elegant evening of cocktails to celebrate. On the invitations, the two explained that although they were changing the parameters of their relationship, their "mutual admiration and caring [was] constant" (Fabrikant 2011).

How to Create Your Own Mindful Divorce Ritual

There's no "right" time to perform a mindful divorce ritual. You might want a ritual to coincide with when you announce or finalize your divorce or when you move into a new house or apartment. You might not want to perform a divorce ritual until years after the fact. Use as your guide what feels right to you and, most important, for your children.

The following are a few simple guidelines for creating a divorce ritual. Remember that the purpose of the ritual is to serve the needs and comfort levels of your children, you, and your ex.

- *Be intentional and explicit.* Let everyone know that this is a sacred moment in your family's life. Normalize divorce as a transition.

- *Be mindful of the ages of the participants.* If you have young children, a fifteen-minute ritual may be long enough. If the ritual is intended to benefit a family of adults, a longer ceremony may be in order.

- *Choose a setting that has meaning.* Natural settings convey permanence in the midst of disruption and change: a beach, the woods, and a mountaintop are some examples. Nature honors the seasons of life.

- *Use objects that are meaningful to you and to the community you invite.* Some examples are photos, candles, bowls of water, open boxes, stones, and children's artwork.

- *Acknowledge loss, and commit to caring.* The centerpiece should be a public or private statement that expresses loss but commits to continuing the care of your children. These are the building blocks of healing.

- *Explicitly express and inspire hopefulness about the future.*
  Divorce is often surrounded with feelings of failure and
  shame. Explicit hopefulness about the future invites healing.

Exercise 9.1 A Storytelling Ritual: Retell Your Divorce Story

The world's oldest ritual is storytelling. Throughout time, people sat around campfires telling the stories of their lives. Even today we are constantly telling stories. Stories that we repeat and that can change in the retelling are rituals that mark our everyday lives. At Thanksgiving in the United States, we retell the story of the early days of this country, sometimes emphasizing the Pilgrims' harsh winters, other times emphasizing their friendship with the Native Americans. You may tell and retell the story of your child's birth or how your family first came to this country. Storytelling offers the opportunity for inner transformation as well as bonding and connection with others, for our stories are at the core of our identities. In telling and revising stories about yourself, you have an opportunity to understand and define yourself anew.

The story of your divorce has great power in your life and a sense of identity. You have probably told your divorce story to a number of people already and will undoubtedly continue with this age-old ritual. Take a moment to make a list of the people you have told.

Now, reflect on your divorce story. Recall the last time you said, "I'm divorced." What emotions did you convey as you related your story about why and how you divorced? Grief, anger, resentment, bitterness, apathy? As I've emphasized throughout this book, naming our emotions helps us cope with them. Beneath the list of people you just listed, write down four to five emotions that went with the story you told them.

What feelings are evoked now as you think about telling your divorce story? In your story of how and why your marriage unraveled or failed, notice who carries the blame, the guilt, or the anger. Reflect on these questions and write a few sentences in your journal.

As your children grow up, they will ask more questions, and you may be called on to offer new information and revise your story. This can be an opportunity for transformation. Here are some questions to ponder:

- Does your story paint your ex or you as a villain?

- Does your story paint your ex or you as a victim?

- Are you telling a story that blames one of you, or do you see a shared responsibility?

- What are the effects of this version of the story? What function does it have? What purpose does it serve?

- Is there a way you can retell this story so that neither of you is a victim or a villain?

Jot down your responses to these questions and look them over. The story of your divorce is part of your identity and legacy. Revising your story of your divorce can be a powerful way to rework your identity and create a more authentic level of befriending. After reading the following story, you may wish to revise the story of your divorce.

• One Couple's Retelling of Their Divorce Story

Rosa came to my office after her fourteen-year-old son, Derek, had failed three subjects at school and was reported for fighting in the lunchroom. Four years earlier, Derek's father, Hando, had left Rosa for their next-door neighbor. Ever since then, she'd portrayed Hando as the villain who was responsible for ruining their marriage. She was the innocent victim, and to right that wrong, Hando was banned from entering Rosa's house. Derek saw his father on weekends. Rosa's emotions spanned the gamut, from feeling furious at her ex to depressed and lonely, to guilty and responsible for Derek's problems.

Although she'd come to my office to address Derek's problems, as Rosa explored her own life, she realized she'd married a man who was far less educated than she was, and she admitted that she had been bored with him and their life together. She had developed her own set of interests and friends, and realized now that she had sought to avoid intimacy with her husband, sexual as well as emotional. In owning her own dissatisfaction, she was able to take responsibility for her part in the dissolution of her marriage. In doing so, she began to see that she was no longer the victim, and Hando was no longer the villain. With this realization came a new round of grief.

"Maybe we were never right for one another in the first place," Rosa said. "I married him to escape my parents' house, but we didn't really have enough in common." She began to realize that blaming her ex not only had consequences for her son, but also was an unfair telling of what had really gone on.

In the next few weeks, Rosa continued to revise the story of her divorce in a way that was less blaming and more forgiving of her ex. She remembered all the ways that she had been critical of, rejecting of, and mean to Hando, and with this came more guilt and regret. "I can understand why Hando found someone else," she admitted. "I won't forget how betrayed I felt, but I do feel less angry."

Next, Rosa set aside time to apologize to her son and retell the story of her divorce to him. "I'm sorry I've been so angry about your papa," she began. "I realize I've not been fair to you. Even though we're not married anymore, Papa has always loved you and always will."

Derek shrugged. "I never want to get married when I grow up," he said.

Rosa said, "I hope you change your mind when you get older. I hope you'll find someone to love who loves you back. That's what it was like with Papa and me at first; we loved each other. But we were too young; we weren't ready for marriage, and even though we were in love, we were not right for each other."

Derek shrugged again and then asked if his father could come over and hang out in his room.

Rosa called Hando and explained that she wanted to move on. She apologized and asked if they could put the past behind them and try to be friendly to one another. When she invited him to a lasagna dinner that Sunday, Hando was taken aback. Sunday-night lasagna had been the family ritual he'd missed the most. He said he'd have to think about it. He didn't accept her invitation at first, but when Rosa invited him again a week later, he agreed. When both parents saw their son doing better in school and making new friends, they decided to reinstate their Sunday lasagna dinners. Much to her surprise, Rosa found herself relaxed enough to laugh and enjoy herself on these occasions.

Interestingly, Rosa came up with a new story about her divorce without actually talking to her ex. It was her inner transformation that allowed her to move forward in befriending. While it's ideal for children if both parents agree on the same story, it's entirely possible to heal from your divorce by working on yourself, without your ex's participation.

The story of your divorce is at the center of your new identity and your new life. With each new telling, you will undoubtedly find new meanings, edit details, and understand new nuances. For children, it's crucial to convey the message that the divorce is not the breakup of the family, but a reorganization of the family across two households. Ultimately, you will construct a new story that does that for you, your children, and, yes, your ex.

Everyday Rituals and Celebrations

We rely on everyday rituals to give our lives order and meaning. A child who demands that a parent recite "Sleep tight; don't let the bedbugs bite" every night before turning out the light is asking to be told that life is reliable and continuous. Delivering the same phrase tonight as last night and previous nights is a reassuring constant in the stressful transitions of divorce. For you and your ex to consciously keep roughly identical but new breakfast, dinner, and bedtime rituals may seem like too much work as you get on with your separate lives, but it's well worth the effort to help your child feel secure.

Everyday rituals remind us of life's joys, rewards, rhythms, and transitions. Going out for ice cream with the kids and your ex after the team wins a game, and spending Saturday mornings sitting on the back steps drinking coffee with your ex while the kids play out back are examples of everyday celebrations that can sweeten life for you, your children, and your ex.

The day that you can see your ex as an ally rather than an adversary, if only for a moment, is transformative. Happy, positive experiences such as celebrating a holiday with your extended binuclear family can transform a group of isolated individuals into a warm community.

Deciding exactly what rituals and celebrations to keep from the "old life" and what to create anew is a task that you may tackle alone or with your befriended ex. Consider this process as ongoing and adjustable, like the relationship you share with your ex. You may choose to observe certain rituals and celebrations as a family and others as single parents.

Keeping Old Rituals and Celebrations

Old rituals create feelings of security, comfort, and continuity, and are especially important in the early stages after divorce. The first question one nine-year-old asked after being told his parents were divorcing was "Will we still have pizza night on Mondays?" Although, at that point, his parents were still contentious, they did manage to go out with their son every Monday to the same pizzeria they'd frequented since he was five years old. The fact that the parents managed to be civil to one another for that hour, that the pizzeria owner greeted them as if everything were "business as usual," and that their son enjoyed his favorite food helped the family weather the worst parts of the separation and served as a stepping-stone to the befriended relationship that the two exes eventually formed.

Think about what rituals you want to keep. Remember that your goal is to befriend your ex and assure your children that you and their other parent are still family.

To get you started, here are some examples: Ginny and James continued to walk their elementary-school-aged children to the bus stop every

Monday morning for the first year they were separated. Erica called their children to say "Good night" when they slept at Steve's house, and Steve did the same when the children slept at Erica's house. Caroline continued to host the end-of-season party for her daughters' soccer team in her backyard, and Marcel came over to work the barbecue. George, an engineer, had always helped Milo, his middle-schooler, with math homework. They continued this arrangement by VoIP (voice over Internet protocol) when Milo stayed at his mother's house.

Creating New Rituals and Celebrations

Instead of living under the same roof with your ex and your children, you are now two separate adults dealing with two households. New rituals and celebrations signal to everyone that life's conditions can still be reliable and secure, notwithstanding the ongoing changes that divorce brings.

Perhaps the most important new ritual is "the switching hour": the time when you and your ex transition the children from one home to another. Regardless of whether this happens weekly, monthly, or yearly, having to say good-bye to one parent and hello to the other parent can be difficult and possibly anxiety producing for children, and it's a time when they need extra assurance. It can also be a difficult time for you and your ex, requiring the same sensitivity toward one another that you offer your children.

Doug and Beth made a concerted effort to create a ritual that communicated family togetherness each Sunday night at the switching hour. For twenty to thirty minutes, they focused solely on the kids. Together, the parents unpacked Ethan's science-project materials and Clara's gymnastics clothing. The parent who was dropping the kids off (often with the kids chiming in) told little stories from the preceding week: Clara had skinned her elbow at recess and gone to see the school nurse, Ethan had hit the winning home run for his baseball team, the new puppy was chewing up the chair legs in the kitchen, and so on. No one talked on the phone or answered e-mails during this time that marked the children's week ending at one parent's house and beginning at the other parent's house. Doug and Beth didn't use this time to hash out any adult issues between themselves. It was a time to intentionally remind the children that their parents could still work as a team. After about a year, Doug and Beth felt comfortable enough to sometimes extend the ritual time by eating dinner together with the kids.

The following are examples of other new rituals:

In chapter 1 you met Jeb and Kim, who created a ritual of sitting down together each August to evaluate how their custody arrangement was working (discussing everything from holiday celebrations to everyday logistics). As the children grew older, they, too, were included in these "family" meetings.

Monday morning, after the kids went to school, was the time Liza and Ernie set aside for phone discussions about settling finances, problems the kids might be having, or schedule changes.

Leanne and Carl both had aging parents. They developed the tradition of celebrating the two sets of grandparents' birthdays with the kids. Together, they would visit the home of the aging parents.

On Super Bowl Sundays, Maureen always had a full house. Gathered in the oversized family room were her teenage sons and their crew of friends, her second husband, *and* her first husband. "What can I say?" Maureen laughed when asked if everyone got along at this annual event. "I married two football fans. Everyone has a great time together, and fortunately they all root for the same team."

Holidays

Holiday celebrations typically undergo many changes when parents divorce. The first years after the divorce can be a tough time as you, the children, and your ex feel the loss of the original family unit. Be prepared to be flexible about holiday arrangements as everyone's needs change.

Some divorced parents agree to alternate specific holidays: "This year the kids are with me on Christmas, next year with you." Other exes divvy up the holidays: "You get the Fourth of July because that's when your extended family has their annual reunion, and I get Memorial Day because that's when I like to take the kids camping." Although it can be wonderful when exes feel warm and comfortable enough to celebrate holidays together, that doesn't usually happen immediately after the divorce, and it doesn't happen for every family. Whatever you decide, the bottom line for holidays is that both your ex and you feel that the arrangement is comfortable and fair.

Holidays Apart

When you choose to celebrate holidays separately, the befriended thing to do is encourage the children to call the absent parent and wish him a happy holiday. Some exes arrange for the children to spend part of the day with each parent. In one interfaith binuclear family I know, the children spend Christmas Eve with their mother, but their father, who is Jewish, comes over on Christmas morning for the opening of presents.

Holidays Together

You may be able to celebrate one holiday with your ex, even if you don't feel up to an extravagant, expanded-clan bash. One of you can take the kids trick-or-treating, and the other can stay home and give out the candy. You can light the candles together for one of the eight nights of Hanukkah. You can drop in for your ex's open-house celebration on New Year's Day.

Vacations

Occasionally, when the children are young, some divorced parents choose to take vacations together. Vacationing together is the exception rather than the rule, so don't push yourself into an uncomfortable arrangement or one that doesn't seem like a good choice for you. If a specific vacation spot is a cherished tradition, and you and your ex are companionable enough to get along in close quarters, it will mean a lot to the kids to have both parents come along. I know divorced parents of toddler twins who vacationed together simply because it was too difficult for one parent to handle both children alone. Other families remember that vacations were their best times together, and the divorced parents still manage to relax and have fun. Bear in mind, however, that vacationing together might allow children to become overly hopeful that their parents will reunite. Be clear that there's no possibility of Daddy and Mommy remarrying.

Celebrations

Befriended exes are able to communicate, compromise, collaborate, and be compassionate toward one another, the four "c's." The fifth "c" is the ability to *celebrate* life's milestones that the exes will continue to share. Remember this ancient saying: "Joy shared, twice the gain; sorrow shared, half the pain." Life offers us moments of joy and sorrow, and these unexpected moments can help you and your ex bond.

Your Child's Birthday

When Jill and Arnie told their children they were separating, eight-year-old Maggie's first question was "Am I still having my birthday party?" Probably no day is more important to most children than their birthday. Finding a way to share your child's birthday celebration is one hallmark of a befriended relationship. To help the day unfold smoothly, be sure to discuss:

- Where the party will be held: at your house, your ex's house, or a more neutral place (such as a park or an ice-skating rink)

- Whether new partners will be included

- Whether you and your ex will buy your child a gift individually or together

- Who will plan the list and take responsibility for the invitees

- How you will handle the cost

The meaning of your child's birthday will change as your child grows up and leaves home. After thirty years of being divorced, Rich still calls his ex-wife on the birthday of each of their three children, now all in their twenties, to thank her for giving birth to them!

Acknowledging Your Ex's Special Days

You can support your ex, and the befriended relationship, by helping your children select gifts for her birthday, Mother's Day, and other significant days. Young children can draw a card. Teenagers can be reminded to purchase a small gift. A small goodwill gesture goes a long way toward befriending your ex.

Milestones: Graduations and Weddings

A friend remarked, "Marriage is transitory; divorce is forever." Befriending your ex takes on new meaning as your children grow up. If you are divorcing or separating with adult children, many new milestones await you. Graduations from nursery school to college are events that both you and your ex will want to attend. If you have young children, the following scenarios may not be ones that you have considered; imagine:

- Your child graduating from kindergarten

- Your child being elected captain of the high-school swim team

- Your child's first day of college

- Your child's wedding

- Attending your child's housewarming

- Your child becoming a parent

- Yourself becoming a grandparent

Jot down some notes about the feelings that are evoked as you imagine these future events.

Throughout this book I've stressed the importance of keeping the big picture in mind: your children's well-being doesn't end when they leave "home." (Technically, in binuclear families, the children will leave two homes when they grow up.) Your ex will be present when and if your children marry and have their own children. Becoming grandparents is a milestone that you will share with your ex. As your children's lives expand, you will attend family events that they host. If you do the hard work of befriending your ex, you will reap many benefits, including being a part of a host of celebratory and joyous milestones. If you and your ex are *not* able to befriend one another, these same milestones will be filled with tension, stress, and emotional challenges.

Take a moment now to review your last journal entry, and think about the events to come. Is there anything you can do now to assure yourself of a brighter future for your family? The following are two possible scenarios of a common event in a child's life.

• Two Marriage Stories

Diana had one of the worst days of her life when her daughter got married. Her ex-husband, Charlie, paid for the wedding but made loud remarks all evening about how Diana was and always had been a cheapskate. Walking on either side of their daughter down the aisle, Diana felt herself breaking out in hives. During the wedding meal, Diana sat at a table at one side of the room with her family, Charlie sat at the other side of the room with his new girlfriend, and their daughter and new son-in-law sat at a third table with their backs to both parents. After the wedding, Diana was sick for a week with a high fever and a terrible case of hives.

That same weekend, across the country, Chiquita had a great time at her daughter's wedding. As Chiquita and her ex-husband, Donald, walked their daughter down the aisle, Chiquita felt her heart swell with love and pride. During the wedding meal, Chiquita sat at a table with her new husband; her ex-husband, Donald; and Donald's new wife. Their new son-in-law had also grown up in a binuclear family of befriended exes who had remarried, so his parents and their new partners composed two more couples. All eight parents had a great time getting to know one another. Later, Chiquita and Donald danced together and remarked with wonder how quickly time had passed since their little girl had been born. Afterward, Chiquita said it had been one of the best days of her life.

As you can see, the exes who remained angry had a terrible experience at their daughter's wedding, whereas the befriended exes were able to enjoy their daughter's special day, support her, and also enjoy their time with one another and their extended families. Keep in mind that you are the architect of your divorce and your life.

Third Parties and Rituals

Sometimes a third party, such as a relative, close friend, or helping professional, can play an integral part in rituals that help divorced partners befriend one another. Third parties can be a buffer between warring exes or messengers between estranged ones. If a relative or friend helps you and your ex with the befriending process, you are a lucky recipient!

The following story illustrates how a relative helped initiate rituals that ultimately helped turn a dysfunctional family into a befriended family.

Eleanor had been divorced from Brent for a little over a year when he married Kristina. Eleanor and Brent's two-year-old son, Benji, lived with Brent during the week and with Eleanor on the weekends. Eleanor was busy with her acting career, and Brent wasn't the communicative type, so their postdivorce relationship was fairly distant. But when Brent married Kristina, Eleanor began to worry about being *too* distant from Benji. She didn't like to call Kristina and Brent's house, because Brent never seemed available and Kristina was cold and abrupt. True to the stereotype, divorce had disconnected this family.

Benji was a rambunctious preschooler, and Kristina was often overwhelmed by his antics. One morning, when she was late for work and racing to get him to day care, Benji had an unbelievable tantrum about putting on his shoes. Kristina, too, began to cry. Marrying Brent was one thing, but she hadn't realized how much child care would be involved. Enter Connie, Kristina's mother, who lived in the same apartment building and happened to drop in. Connie made short work of getting Benji's shoes on, and whisked him off to day care. Thus began a new set of morning rituals between Granny Connie and little Benji that would eventually help this clan to befriend.

Next, Connie offered herself as a "bridge" between Benji's two families. She suggested they use her apartment for what had been stressful drop-offs and pickups between Benji's two families. With this new set of "switching hour" rituals, Connie got to know and like Eleanor.

One evening, when Eleanor called Connie to let her know she was running late, Kristina picked up the phone. The two women began a lengthy conversation about their shared interest: Benji. Before long, Connie, Kristina, and Eleanor found themselves frequently putting their heads together to solve the everyday problems of managing this active three-year-old, who had been recently diagnosed with attention deficiencies.

A domino effect had begun. As Kristina became more comfortable with Eleanor, she encouraged her husband, Brent, to reconnect with his ex. Once Eleanor and Brent thawed toward one another, they could heal the place in their hearts the pain of divorce had torn open, and create a new and loving expanded family. Benji now had four people (Brent, Eleanor, Kristina, and Connie) who cared deeply about him. And this reality had all sorts of practical implications. Benji spent most Mother's Days and many other holidays in the company of his father, his biological mother, his stepmother, and his step-grandmother. And the domino effect continued: ironically, when Brent was in one of his difficult workaholic phases, it was Eleanor who helped Kristina understand him better!

Conclusion

Deciding exactly what rituals and celebrations to keep from your "old life" and how and when to create new ones is a task that befriended exes must take on. Having befriended parents can reassure the children in important moments, from the "switching hour" to children's birthdays. Befriending your ex means that a host of future holidays and children's milestones will be celebratory and joyous for you, your children, and your ex.

You may be thinking, *I've made a lot of progress since I began reading this book, but I'm still not exactly friends with my ex! Is there hope?* There's always hope. Befriending, just like divorce, is not a one-time event but an unfolding process.

The final chapter includes a "must have" list of tips for encouraging a long-term befriended relationship with your ex. This list, along with some more befriending stories, may also give you hope that it's always possible to befriend your ex, even if it has been many years since your divorce.

CHAPTER 10

is it ever too late to befriend your ex?

When Betsy first learned that her twenty-five-year-old son, Bobby, had invited his father, Stuart, to his upcoming wedding, she thought she would explode with anger and anxiety. Stuart had been estranged from Betsy and the kids since the divorce twenty years earlier. She'd worked hard, remarried, and raised the kids, while her ex had sent an occasional Christmas card, each time with a new return address. And now he was going to just show up! Whenever Betsy thought about seeing Stuart again, she felt a host of unpleasant feelings surfacing: resentment that he hadn't contributed a dime to child support, loss about his absence when the kids were growing up, apprehension that his presence at the wedding events would be disruptive, and fear that he'd somehow wreck the new life she'd carefully built.

Although it didn't happen immediately, the wedding transformed Betsy's relationship with her ex. First, she had to tell her extended family and friends that Stuart was coming. That gave her a lot of opportunities to talk things out. She saw the happy transformation in Bobby as he and Stuart got to know one another through e-mails and phone calls. Although meeting again was awkward at first, she felt touched and proud when Stuart asked to speak to her privately and told her she'd done a great job of raising their son. When Bobby and his wife said their vows, Betsy looked over at Stuart, saw the tears in his eyes, and was surprised at how moved she felt to be sharing these special moments with her son's father. Ultimately, the rehearsal dinner, the ceremony and celebration, and the "day-after party" gave Betsy and her ex a neutral place where the ice around her heart began to thaw and she was able to reconnect, let go, forgive, and befriend.

Befriending Is Always a Possibility

Even when befriending is impossible immediately after the divorce, with time the possibility may become more viable, and it remains a valuable endeavor. Even if you have been divorced for a long time and are estranged from your ex, it's not too late to befriend. Research (Ahrons 1994, 2004; Emery 2004, Hetherington and Kelly 2002; Wallerstein, Lewis, and Blakeslee 2000) has found that it's not only young or school-age children who suffer when their divorced parents are opponents. Adult children benefit enormously when their parents are on good terms, and this includes adult children who lived through the divorce as children as well as those who are encountering it now. These adult children no longer have to hold secrets from one parent, feel torn apart for caring for a "victim" or loving a "villain," or function as a mediator between the two parents. Adult children, even those who have their own busy lives, can feel underlying sadness, depression, and anxiety when their divorced parents are estranged or enemies (Marquardt 2005; Staal 2000).

Life is long. People can change. Although there comes a point when it no longer makes sense to *actively* try to befriend your ex—for example, if he is resistant or continually angry, or she is too debilitated by personal problems, such as addiction—bear in mind that just because you are not friends right now doesn't mean you won't be friends at some point in the future. The story of Betsy and Stuart reminds me of how often people who were once married can be open to and welcome reconnection, even after many years of separation and bitterness. It reminds me that no matter how ugly a divorce, compassion and forgiveness are always possibilities, as in the following examples.

Although Henrietta and Yor had remained businesslike—cordial but distant from one another after their divorce—years later, when Yor married Georgia, he deliberately invited his ex,

Henrietta, to participate in his marriage. He included her in the service with a prayer: "I bless you, Henrietta, for all that you opened me and our children to in our seven years together, especially your loving extended family and your family's love of nature and music."

Several years after her divorce, Rheba was diagnosed with cancer. Although she and her ex had often argued bitterly since the divorce, when he learned of her unfortunate news, he immediately called her to offer his support. She was particularly touched by the support of his new wife, Moira, a cancer survivor, who tearfully wished Rheba well and offered, "Let me know if there is any way I can help while you are recovering. Please call me anytime."

At the wedding of his son, Raul, Ben's ex-wife and Raul's mother, Beti, publicly thanked Ben's current wife for the love and guidance she'd given Raul. This was Ben's moment of transformation: for the first time in many years, he didn't freeze up and automatically discount Beti. Instead, he felt warm toward his ex-wife. The two sets of parents (Beti, too, had remarried) shared a first dance with Raul and his wife.

Unfortunately there are times when reaching out doesn't always work so well. The following is an example of an attempt at befriending that backfired.

When Befriending Is Impossible Right Now

After hearing a talk on divorced parents and collaborative child rearing, forty-four-year-old Alice contacted her ex, Peter. They'd divorced two decades earlier and had rarely had any contact, but the seminar had awakened some of Alice's dormant feelings of shame and regret as she realized how deeply scarred her children had been by the acrimony of their divorce, which included bitter financial and legal battles as well as vicious parental abduction incidents. She wrote her ex, Peter, the following letter, admitting to her vulnerable feelings and reaching out for healing:

Dear Peter,

I wish we had been able to do things differently during the past twenty years. Looking back, I believe we became enemies without realizing what the consequences would be for our children. Speaking for myself, I was too young, ignorant, and powerless to understand how our decisions or *my* lack of decisions, which I see now as being totally irresponsible, would affect the children. What we went through not only affected *me*, but also damaged our children—and has resulted in fallout for the rest of all our lives.

I'm aware that you may feel differently, but I live with daily regrets regarding how our actions caused them so much pain and suffering. I'm now so aware that the lack of consistency and safety damaged them, as well as our disregard for so many things that really mattered (like the total fragmentation of their education). Even though the kids are grown now, might it be possible for you and me to heal part of the chasm between us? After all, we will soon become grandparents.

With regrets in these matters,

Alice

Simply writing the letter had gotten Alice in touch with all that she longed for, for herself and her children. It made her aware that the hurt she felt over what had happened long ago was still eating at her, as was her enormous guilt for what she and Peter had put their children through. She hoped to open a conversation with Peter about the past. Maybe he was feeling the same way as she did? But the letter she received from Peter was not what she'd hoped for.

Alice:

I have no idea what you are talking about.
In any case, guilt and regrets serve little purpose today.
Everyone does the best they can in child rearing.

Peter

When Alice read Peter's response, her heart sank. She felt stung. She could easily imagine his critical, dismissive voice, and was amazed at how disappointed and rejected she felt. After all these years, she hadn't expected to still be vulnerable to her ex. But his response made it clear that they couldn't reconnect in any meaningful way. She realized that she would have to do any healing of the past on her own, without her ex's cooperation.

Her first impulse was to call her children to tell them what a loser their father still was, but fortunately she controlled her reaction to her anger and hurt. Instead, she talked with a close friend about the impact of Peter's rejection and her sense of ongoing loss. Only after a great deal of soul searching, during which she revisited the painful events in her past, was Alice able to let go and find compassion and forgiveness for herself.

If you have tried and tried your best, and decided that befriending is impossible, congratulate yourself for trying, and don't take your ex's inability to reciprocate as a personal rejection. Perhaps the best you can do is accept a limited befriended relationship—for now. Maybe you can keep the door open, if only a crack, to the idea that befriending may be possible in the future.

Keeping the Door Open to Befriending

I bought my second husband a book for our thirteenth wedding anniversary, *5 Simple Steps to Take Your Marriage from Good to Great*, by Terri Orbuch (2009). Three habits the author recommends developing to keep a marriage strong are relevant to strengthening your relationship with your befriended ex:

- *Expect less, get more.* This means keeping your goals realistic, and seeing the good and praising it.

- *Give incentives and rewards.* Do and say simple things to show your ex appreciation. The most important phrases in all languages are "Please," "Thank you," "I'm sorry," "I forgive you," and "Please forgive me."

- *Keep costs low, benefits high.* Audit your behavior. Weed out the costly, unprofitable actions.

Orbuch's book (ibid.) reminded me that the destructive and damaging behaviors of a marriage are likely to remain in a divorce unless you make a mindful, determined effort to eliminate, correct, or repair them.

The following are some specific recommendations to follow to keep the door open to a befriended relationship. Even if you are already observing many of these recommendations, it's worthwhile to review them:

- Compliment your ex on something ordinary: "Thanks for bringing the kids home on time. Knowing I can count on your being prompt makes my life run smoothly."

- Compliment your ex on something special: "The kids loved that pizza you brought in last week!"

- Remind your children to remember your ex's special days: "Did you remember Mom's birthday? May I take you to get a gift or card for Father's Day?"

- Practice anger management. Remind yourself to breathe if you feel a shout welling up; count to ten or think *Red light.*

- Listen empathetically, in a way that encourages your ex to speak. Practice active listening. When you feel an urge to respond, count to ten or think Red light, and encourage your ex to keep talking.

- Apologize when you make a mistake: "I'm so sorry I got the kids to you so late; I hadn't predicted the traffic."

- Teach your children to be compassionate and kind to your ex: "Remember to take good care of your father; he just had dental surgery."

- Create new rituals. Invite your ex to join you at a dinner to celebrate one of the children's birthdays or a good report card.

- Honor old rituals. Invite your ex's sister or brother to one of the children's family celebrations.

- Practice gratitude: "Thank you for reminding the kids about my birthday (or Mother's Day)."

- Offer support: "I know how hard it is to get Josh to go to sleep. Let me tell you what worked for me last week."

- Offer empathy: "I, too, feel terrible when I yell at Johnny when he won't take his medicine, but sometimes I can't help it!"

- Keep the communication channels open: "Call me whenever you feel as if you are losing it with them."

- Develop compassion for your ex. Consciously remember the positive qualities and strengths you admired in your ex when you first met.

If these behaviors are already part of your daily life, congratulations! You are well on your way to a befriended relationship! If you haven't yet befriended your ex, making these behaviors a habitual part of your daily life increases the likelihood that you and your ex will become and remain friends.

The Triumph of Love over Hate: The Gift of Befriending

When Paul left Renetta and remarried to a neighbor, their children were six, eight, and eleven. For many years Renetta was consumed with a story of bitterness: *How could he have done this to* me? *What did I do to deserve this: being abandoned, left penniless, humiliated, and without a career?* She returned to school and trained as a nurse, which, to her surprise, was both rewarding and lucrative. To his credit, Paul did stay involved in the children's lives, and although negotiating a "limited befriending" wasn't easy for Renetta, she knew that his participation meant a lot to the children. When Paul's second wife left him for a woman, Renetta was gleeful. "He deserves just what he got," she said repeatedly. But when, at age fifty-six, Paul received a diagnosis of terminal cancer, everyone, including Renetta, was surprised that she invited him into her home, where she and their three children took care of him, driving him to chemotherapy and sitting with him through his passing.

When asked why she chose this and how she was able to do it, Renetta replied, "When I heard his diagnosis, something deep within me cracked open. I was filled with sadness. I guess, in the end, love trumped hate. I knew that my kids wanted to care for him, and I knew that this was right. But what surprised me was that I was able to access the feelings I'd had when we fell in love, when we were first married. He'd really been a good husband then."

Let's look at these words again: "I guess, in the end, love trumped hate." Renetta was a blessed woman. As you read earlier in this book, when you access feelings of love, altruism, and compassion, your body releases oxytocin and you are filled with feelings of well-being, even euphoria. Anger and resentment, even when justified, threaten you physically and psychologically by releasing an excess of adrenaline, the stress hormone, throughout your body. Being able to tap into forgiveness, kindness, and generosity fortifies your entire being, both chemically and spiritually. If you are divorced, befriending your ex is one of the pathways to renewal.

Finding a Therapist If You Are Still Having Trouble Befriending

We've covered a lot of territory in this book. You've been introduced to the two important mind-sets that guide befriending (keeping the big picture in mind and taking the high road); skills for regulating grief, anger, and other difficult emotions; and the art of letting go. Whew! If you are feeling stuck or too frustrated to continue the work of befriending, before giving up perhaps you will consider getting some additional support. Befriending does demand a lot of energy and commitment, and a therapist or mental health professional can be extremely helpful.

Mental health professionals include psychiatrists, psychologists, social workers, marriage and family counselors, pastoral counselors, and a variety of other professional counselors and coaches. Finding someone who is licensed assures you that this person is credentialed, but what's more important than the specific category or professional label is finding someone who is qualified and experienced, and in whom you feel confident. Here are some suggestions for finding a mental health professional:

- Ask for referrals from your medical doctors, your child's pediatrician, your child's school counselor, and even your divorce lawyer. Your health insurance company should have a list of mental health providers that are covered.

- Many experienced therapists say that the best way to find a good therapist is by word of mouth. Satisfied customers can tell you a lot about the quality of the therapy you will receive. Although you might be embarrassed to ask friends and family members for recommendations, you may be surprised at how many people you know have sought and been helped by mental health professionals.

- Search the Internet. Type in "Find a therapist" or "How to find a therapist," and you will find many reliable online directories that sort by zip code, specialization, fees, and more specifications. Therapists often offer a small description online conveying in their own words how they work, which can help you get a sense of what the person is like.

- Ideally, you should have three to five phone numbers of professionals to call. Most therapists will talk to you for five to ten minutes on the phone before you decide to make an appointment.

- Trust your intuition. Chemistry, or feeling a comfortable connection with the therapist, is essential. You may be satisfied with the first person you meet, or you may want to meet two to three additional therapists. Don't be afraid to ask questions. Ask therapists how much experience they have in working with people who are divorced and determined to get along with and befriend their exes. You may want to try things out by having two or three sessions before making a firm commitment.

- Be realistic about geography and finances. Find someone who is geographically accessible. Keep your finances in mind. Determine whether you need to find a provider on your health insurance plan or can afford to go outside your plan. Also, inquire whether the therapist is willing to negotiate a sliding payment scale.

- If therapy isn't helping you, discuss this with your therapist. If you're hesitant to have such a discussion, take a risk, push yourself, and initiate this conversation before leaving your next session. Being direct with your therapist may teach you a lot about being direct with your ex!

Conclusion

In this chapter you have seen that befriending can be possible even years after a divorce is finalized. Sometimes, however, befriending is impossible. When this is the case, the best solution may be knowing that you've done your best and then being able to let go.

epilogue

Befriending Your Ex after Divorce is built on the bittersweet premise that a befriended ex is one of the secrets to a divorced person's happiness. I deliberately use the word "bittersweet," because in all likelihood, when you married you never thought you'd be getting divorced, and when you divorced, you probably never thought you would be creating a befriended relationship with your ex, one that would offer you support and nurturing.

Befriending is never finished, because relationships are always changing and growing, just as you are. This book has offered you a variety of tools for befriending. The tools are simple yet complex—that is, difficult to master. They require commitment, determination, the willingness to take a risk and fail, and, above all, practice. Working at mastering these skills is well worth the effort, for they will help you with befriending your ex and beyond. Mastering mindfulness, managing your emotional responses, and being able to keep two mind-sets in the front of your mind—prioritizing the big picture and taking the high road—have the power to change not only your relationship with your ex, but also other relationships. These tools have the power to transform *you*.

Befriending is not a science but an art. You are unique; so is your ex, and so is every moment. No one skill will work for you all the time. What's most important is finding the correct strategy for each unique moment. Honor the five "c's" because they are the backbone of a befriended relationship: communication, collaboration, compromise, compassion, and celebration. As your journey continues, review your journal. You have a host of new tools and skills to help you continue to create the changes you desire, and move forward.

As I write the final sentences of this book, I want to thank you, my readers. I hope that reading this book has given you the gift that writing it has brought me: the gift of self-awareness. Take this moment to congratulate yourself for the work you have already done. You may well find other relationships improving as you make the five "c's" a habit. Enjoy the journey ahead!

APPENDIX

questionnaire used in the befriending interviews

The interviews were open ended, and the questions served only as guidelines. All interviews were conducted face to face or by telephone, e-mail, or VoIP (voice over Internet protocol).

1. Biographical data: What is your current marital status? What year did you marry? Divorce? After how many years of marriage? Did you have any marriages, divorces, or separations prior to this divorce; if so, please explain. How many years have you been divorced?

2. How old were your children when you separated or divorced? How old are they now? List their names and ages, and describe your relationship with them.

3. Judith Wallerstein (2010) states that while it takes two to marry, it only takes one to divorce: "It is rare for both parents to agree on whether to divorce. Typically in a marriage with children, one person wants out, and the other, realizing that there is no choice, goes along, often far more reluctantly than people know." Would you say that your divorce was initiated by you or your ex, or was it a mutual decision?

4. Describe your living arrangements at the time of the divorce: Did you move out of the home you shared with your ex? Did your ex move out? Did both of you move out? (For example: "We sold our home, and the children lived with each of us in our new apartments for one week at a time and switched homes every Sunday night," "I stayed at our family home, and the children lived with me and spent Wednesday and every other weekend with their dad, who moved three blocks away.")

5. Think back to when you divorced: can you sum up in a few sentences how you felt about your relationship with your ex?

6. Most divorces bring out the worst in people and often contain some adversarial experiences that we would like to forget. Do any examples of you and your ex at your worst come to mind? Describe them.

7. How does your current relationship with your ex resemble, or differ from, the one you had in the throes of splitting up? In the immediate aftermath? Please describe one example of how you behaved back then and another of how you behave toward each other now, both characterizing your relationship at these two different points in time.

8. Relationships are always changing, sometimes for the better, sometimes for the worse. Can you describe one or two moments that stand out as turning points, that moved you and your ex subtly or profoundly from being adversaries (your worst selves) to allies (your best selves), or vice versa?

9. Many divorced people feel intimate (nonsexually) in a wide variety of ways with their exes. Can you describe a moment of intimacy between you and your ex that makes you feel that your ex is your ally?

10. Did you ever, or do you now, want more of a friendship with your ex, or vice versa?

11. Answer this question only if it applies: What internal and external obstacles (for example, "I'm depressed," "My ex is an alcoholic") did you have to face to move from being adversaries to being allies?

12. Many times, exes share a devotion and dedication to their children that they don't share with anyone else, including their current partners or spouses. Exes may even enjoy talking about children and old times, and catching up on shared friendships and interests. Is this true for you? Have you ever felt guilty about these feelings vis-à-vis your current partner or your children?

13. What do you know now that you wish you'd known when you were first getting divorced?

references

Ahrons, Constance. 1994. *The Good Divorce: Keeping Your Family Together When Your Marriage Comes Apart.* New York: HarperCollins.

———. 2004. *We're Still Family: What Grown Children Have to Say about Their Parents' Divorce.* New York: HarperCollins.

Baker, Dan, and Cameron Stauth. 2003. *What Happy People Know: How the New Science of Happiness Can Change Your Life for the Better.* Emmaus, PA: Rodale.

Behary, Wendy. 2008. *Disarming the Narcissist: Surviving and Thriving with the Self-Absorbed.* Oakland, CA: New Harbinger Publications.

Blau, Melinda. 1993. *Families Apart: 10 Keys to Successful Coparenting.* New York: Berkley Publishing Group.

Baum, Nehami. 2004. "On Helping Divorced Men to Mourn Their Losses." *American Journal of Psychotherapy* 58 (2):174–85.

Bonanno, George A. 2004. "Loss, Trauma, and Human Resilience: Have We Underestimated the Human Capacity to Thrive after Extremely Aversive Events?" *American Psychologist* 59 (1):20–28.

Bradshaw, John. 1988. *Healing the Shame That Binds You.* Deerfield Beach, FL: Health Communications.

Conroy, Pat, and Becky Johnston. 1991. *The Prince of Tides*. Directed by Barbra Streisand. Culver City, CA: Columbia Pictures.

Emery, Robert E. 2004. *The Truth about Children and Divorce: Dealing with the Emotions So You and Your Children Can Thrive*. New York: Viking.

Fabrikant, Geraldine. 2011. "Divorce, in Style." *New York Times*, May 13. http://www.nytimes.com/2011/05/15/fashion/celebrating-a-divorce-with-a-party-noticed.html

Fisher, Helen. 2004. *Why We Love: The Nature and Chemistry of Romantic Love*. New York: Henry Holt and Company.

Fosha, Diana. 2000. *The Transforming Power of Affect: A Model for Accelerated Change*. New York: Basic Books.

Frank, Anne. 1995. *Diary of a Young Girl*. Edited by Otto H. Frank and Mirjam Pressler. Translated by Susan Massotty. New York: Doubleday.

Freud, Sigmund. 1922. *Beyond the Pleasure Principle*. Edited by Ernest Jones. Translated by C. J. M. Hubback. London: The International Psycho-Analytical Press.

Frost, Robert. 1972. *The Robert Frost Reader: Poetry and Prose*. Edited by Edward Connery Lathem and Lawrance Thompson. New York: Henry Holt and Company.

Gilligan, Carol. 1982. *In a Different Voice: Psychological Theory and Women's Development*. Cambridge: Harvard University Press.

Goldstein, Elisha. 2012. *The Now Effect: How a Mindful Moment Can Change the Rest of Your Life*. New York: Simon and Schuster.

Goleman, Daniel. 1995. *Emotional Intelligence: Why It Can Matter More Than IQ*. New York: Bantam Books.

———. 2006. *Social Intelligence: The New Science of Human Relationships*. New York: Bantam Books.

Gottman, John. 1994. *Why Marriages Succeed or Fail: And How You Can Make Yours Last*. New York: Fireside.

Hanson, Rick. 2009. *Buddha's Brain: The Practical Neuroscience of Happiness, Love, and Wisdom*. Oakland, CA: New Harbinger Publications.

Hetherington, E. Mavis, and John Kelly. 2002. *For Better or Worse: Divorce Reconsidered*. New York: W. W. Norton and Company.

Janov, Arthur. 1970. *The Primal Scream: Primal Therapy—The Cure for Neurosis*. New York: Putnam.

Jong, Erica. 2006. "A Twenty-First Century Ritual." In *Why I'm Still Married: Women Write Their Hearts Out on Love, Loss, Sex, and Who Does the Dishes*, edited by Karen Propp and Jean Trounstine, 75–80. New York: Hudson Street Press.

Kabat-Zinn, Jon. 2012. *Mindfulness for Beginners*. Boulder, CO: Sounds True.

Lavender, Neil, and Alan Cavaiola. 2010. *The One-Way Relationship Workbook*. Oakland, CA: New Harbinger Publications.

———. 2012. *Impossible to Please: How to Deal with Perfectionist Coworkers, Controlling Spouses, and Other Incredibly Critical People*. Oakland, CA: New Harbinger Publications.

Leick, Nini, and Marianne Davidsen-Nielsen. 1991. *Healing Pain: Attachment, Loss, and Grief Therapy*. Translated from Danish by David Stoner. New York: Routledge.

Lerner, Harriet. 1985. *The Dance of Anger: A Woman's Guide to Changing the Patterns of Intimate Relationships*. New York: Harper and Row.

Libet, Benjamin. 2004. *Mind Time: The Temporal Factor in Consciousness*. Cambridge, MA: Harvard University Press.

Marquardt, Elizabeth. 2005. *Between Two Worlds: The Inner Lives of Children of Divorce*. New York: Three Rivers Press.

Miller, Jean Baker. 1976. *Toward a New Psychology of Women*. Boston: Beacon Press.

Moore, Jane. 2006. *The Second Wives Club*. New York: Broadway Books.

Naparstek, Belleruth. 1994. *Staying Well with Guided Imagery*. New York: Warner Books.

Orbuch, Terri L. 2009. *5 Simple Steps to Take Your Marriage from Good to Great*. New York: Delacorte Press.

Paleg, Kim, and Matthew McKay. 2001. *When Anger Hurts Your Relationship: 10 Simple Solutions for Couples Who Fight*. Oakland, CA: New Harbinger Publications.

Pennebaker, James W. 1997. *Opening Up: The Healing Power of Expressing Emotions*. New York: The Guilford Press.

Schab, Lisa. 2008. *The Divorce Workbook for Children*. Oakland, CA: Instant Help Books.

———. 2008. *The Divorce Workbook for Teens*. Oakland, CA: Instant Help Books.

Siegel, Daniel. 2010. *Mindsight: The New Science of Personal Transformation*. New York: Bantam.

Staal, Stephanie. 2000. *The Love They Lost: Living with the Legacy of Our Parents' Divorce*. New York: Delta.

United States Department of Labor. 2012. "Equal Pay," http://www.dol.gov/equalpay, accessed June 7.

Wallerstein, Judith. 2010. "The Blog: If Divorce Is No Fault, Why Do They Fight?" *Huffington Post*, December 16. http://huffingtonpost.com/judith-wallerstein/if-divorce-is-no-fault-wh_b_797310.html.

Wallerstein, Judith S., and Sandra Blakeslee. 1989. *Second Chances: Men, Women, and Children a Decade after Divorce*. New York: Ticknor and Fields.

———. 2003. *What about the Kids? Raising Your Children Before, During, and After Divorce*. New York: Hyperion.

Wallerstein, Judith S., Julia M. Lewis, and Sandra Blakeslee. 2000. *The Unexpected Legacy of Divorce: The 25 Year Landmark Study*. New York: Hyperion.

Woolf, Virginia. 1976. "A Sketch of the Past." In *Moments of Being: Unpublished Autobiographical Writings*, edited, and with introduction and notes, by Jeanne Schulkind, 61–160. New York: Harcourt Brace Jovanovich.

Worden, William J. 2009. *Grief Counseling and Grief Therapy: A Handbook for the Mental Health Practitioner*. 4th ed. New York: Springer Publishing Company.

Worthington, Everett L. Jr. 1998. "The Pyramid Model of Forgiveness: Some Interdisciplinary Speculations about Unforgiveness and the Power of Forgiveness." In *Dimensions of Forgiveness: Psychological Research and Theological Perspectives*, edited by Everett L. Worthington, Jr., 107–139. Radnor, PA: Templeton Foundation Press.

Judith Ruskay Rabinor, PhD, is author of A *Starving Madness* and founder and director of the American Eating Disorders Center of Long Island. Divorced over twenty-five years ago, Rabinor has since remarried and has successfully co-parented her two grown children.

Foreword writer Don-David Lusterman, PhD, is a licensed psychologist in private practice in Baldwin, NY, and author of *Infidelity: A Survival Guide*.

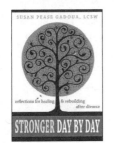

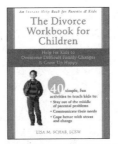